The Life and Adventures of John Nicol, Mariner

D0587191

The Life and Adventures of John Nicol, Mariner

Edited and with an Introduction
by Tim Flannery

Canongate

First published in Great Britain in 2000 by
Canongate Books Ltd, 14 High Street
Edinburgh EH1 ITE

10 9 8 7 6 5 4 3 2 1

Introduction and editing of this edition copyright © Tim
Flannery, 1997

First published in 1822
Published in 1997 by The Text Publishing Company,
Melbourne, Australia
This edition first published in 1997 by Atlantic Monthly Press,
New York
The author gratefully acknowledges Edward Stanley for his
advice on naval history

The moral right of the author has been asserted

British Library Cataloguing-in-Publication Data
A catalogue record for this book is available on
request from the British Library

ISBN 1 84195 091 2

Printed and bound by Omnia Books Limited, Glasgow

Contents

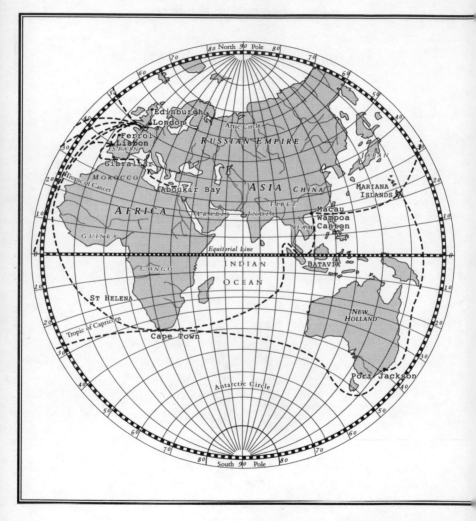

Map of the world as Nicol would have

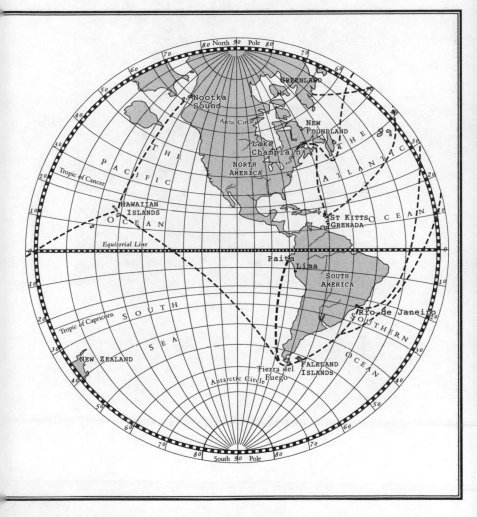

known it, showing some of his journeys.

JOHN NICOL
MARINER, AGE 67

Introduction

by Tim Flannery

J OHN NICOL TWICE circled the globe, in the
process visiting all six habitable continents.
He fought American revolutionaries and Napoleon's
navy, was in Hawaii when Cook's murderers were still
young, in Port Jackson when Sydney consisted of
about a thousand souls, and in the West Indies when
African slaves were beginning to experiment with the
music which would become blues and jazz. In short,
as he roamed the world in the late eighteenth century,
he saw the modern age in its infancy.

The world John Nicol records is not one of admi-
rals, governors and high officials, for he was by his
own admission a simple 'bungs'—an 'unlettered'
cooper. He describes a world seen from below decks;
a world peopled by slaves, convicts and Chinese
barbers, many of whom Nicol counted among his
friends. As such, his story is an extreme rarity. People
like Nicol usually lacked the means to have their
adventures recorded, and publishers were largely
uninterested in such autobiographies. Indeed, a significant fraction of Nicol's compatriots would not

even have lived to tell their stories. When he sailed, mortality rates of 15 per cent *per annum* were not looked upon as especially bad, yet Nicol survived twenty-five years at sea.[1]

The story of how this book came into existence is almost as remarkable as the one Nicol himself tells. Picture yourself in a street in Edinburgh with the freezing winter of 1822 just beginning to relax its grip. An old derelict totters feebly along, picking tiny fragments of coal from between the icy cobbles. These he places in the pocket of an old apron tied round his waist. They will be used to light a small fire, over which he will crouch, trying to fight off the chill. As he searches for his coals, the old man is approached by a 'very strange person' and so begins the encounter which, after a long and happenstance history, places this book in your hands today.[2]

The 'very strange person' was John Howell, who was to record and edit Nicol's work. Even in nineteenth-century Scotland Howell was an anomaly. He described himself as a 'polyartist'. Although a bookbinder by trade, he was an inveterate inventor and tinkerer by nature. The most enduring of his contrivances is the 'plough', a device used by bookbinders

1 Simmons, J. J. (III), 'Those Vulgar Tubes', *Studies in Nautical Archaeology* no. 1, Department of Archaeology, Texas University, 1991.
2 Nicol, John, *The Life and Adventures of John Nicol, Mariner, with a foreword and afterword by Alexander Laing*, Cassell & Company, London, 1937, 27.

well into the present century. Alexander Laing, who gave some biographical notes on Howell, remarked of this invention that 'many a careless binder has ruined good books by too exuberant cropping [with it].'[1]

Howell's other inventions included 'a reliable salve for the ringworm' and a method for the fabrication of false teeth. Transport also intrigued him. He invented a flying machine (the testing of which, from the roof of an old tannery, cost him a broken leg), and a sort of prototype submarine. This latter nearly led to fratricide, for John encouraged an unwilling brother to enter the 'large model of a fish' for its test run on the River Leith. The brother refused, however, and John took his place. A contemporary account reports that:

> Scarcely had the fish entered the water when it capsized: the keel turning upwards, and poor John was submerged. Sounds of an alarming kind were heard to issue from the belly of the fish, and no time was lost in dragging it to the bank, when the inventor was liberated from his perilous position; but it took nearly half an hour before 'suspended animation' was fully restored.[2]

Howell's other great interest lay in the exploits of military men and adventurers. He published five books, three of which concerned such people. The first, *Journal of a Soldier of the 71st, or Glasgow Regiment* was followed by *The Life and Adventures of John Nicol, Mariner* and,

1 *Life and Adventures*, 1937, 26.
2 ibid., 28.

finally, *The Life of Alexander Alexander Written by Himself*. Howell's method seems to have consisted of befriending old soldiers and sailors, then spending months writing down or editing their life stories. One wonders whether they moved into his house for the duration. Whatever the case, Howell's motives were noble ones, for he signed over royalties to his adoptees, and endeavoured to use their stories to obtain for them their well deserved pensions.

Howell's 1822 edition of *The Life and Adventures of John Nicol, Mariner* is a modest little book, measuring just sixteen centimetres by ten. Its only illustration is a simple drawing of Nicol himself—in all probability placed there to evoke the reader's pity. It shows the weatherbeaten and wistful countenance of one who has seen much of life. The book's rarity now suggests that the print run was small. Its only republication occurred in 1937 when Cassell issued an edition 'embellished with numerous original designs' by Gordon Grant, and with a foreword and afterword by Laing, who claims that *Life and Adventures* is the earliest reminiscence by an ordinary sailor that 'has any claim to permanence as literature'. The book, he says, 'acquainted me ... with a distinct personality I should have felt far the poorer for not having known, and from time to time I have sought him out again, in his book, with the same pleasure I should take in looking up an old friend.'

John Nicol had 'seen more of the world than most persons in Edinburgh, perhaps in Britain' according to Howell, yet throughout his life he seems to have remained almost unworldly. This may stem from the fact that, like many seamen, he led a largely sheltered life. While at sea, his domestic and financial arrangements were made for him. Decisions were made by others, and there was little time for romance with all its complications. In these ways, going to sea was akin to joining a religious order.

Nicol was not a sailor of the rum, sodomy and the lash school. When he first went to sea he read his Bible daily and it troubled his conscience that he lost the habit. He was shy, did not drink heavily and was appalled by foul language. At times one wonders how this good and simple man mixed it with the recurrent brutality of life at sea.

Nicol's naivety shows through nowhere more clearly than in his first romance. After meeting a young woman on a coach journey he feels 'something uncommon arise in [his] breast'. After a number of efforts, he 'summonsed the resolution to take her hand in mine; I pressed it gently, she drew faintly back'. With little more encouragement than that, Nicol decides upon marriage and, were it not for a recalcitrant prospective father-in-law, may have succeeded in his designs. He was equally 'at sea' with the most important female in his life, a convict girl named Sarah Whitlam who became his great love. Yet time has shown that his assessment of Sarah Whitlam was hardly an accurate one.

Given the editorial role Howell played, one

wonders how much of *The Life and Adventures of John Nicol, Mariner* represents his input, for the beauty of the language sometimes makes the reader doubt whether it could be the work of an unlettered cooper. Laing speculates that Howell's influence on the book's style and content was minor. He notes that the two works published by Howell alone (*An Essay upon the War Galleys of the Ancients* and *The Life and Adventures of Alexander Selkirk*) 'lack the passages of terse grandeur which lifts Nicol's story, from time to time, to the level of great English prose'.[1] Howell was also a great respecter of facts, and is unlikely to have tampered with the subjects of Nicol's work. Nicol himself says that he will make his story as interesting as is in his power, 'consistent with truth'; its detail is in itself a guide to its authenticity. He remembers, for instance, how Chinese washer women kept a pig in 'a cage-like box fixed to the stern of their sampan.' On the Falkland Islands the geese he saw were 'very pretty, spreckled like a partridge.'

There is something very special about Nicol's prose, with its attention to minute detail, recalled decades after the events occurred. Perhaps this derives from Nicol's style, which is clearly in the great oral storytelling tradition of the sea, owing more to the long tradition of the storytelling bards than to the written prose of his contemporaries. The natural

1 *Life and Adventures*, 1937, 23.

rhythm and pattern of such language is a powerful aid to memory. The stories, told over and over, become ever more refined and compelling. Nicol even draws a picture of himself as raconteur, late in his life, when he takes a boat to London to attempt to gain his pension: 'I was at sea again ... I had always a crowd round me listening to my accounts of the former voyages that I had made ... I was very happy.' From such stories has come this vivid and romantic tale of travel to the hidden corners of the world.

A large part of the fascination of Nicol's book lies in his service as steward aboard the *Lady Juliana* transport which, as part of the second fleet, brought over two hundred female convicts to Australia in 1790. The logbook of the *Lady Juliana* is long lost, so Nicol's account is the main source of information for the voyage.[1] His time aboard the *Lady Juliana* (which he recollects as the *Lady Julian*) was formative, for Nicol fell in love with a convict girl named Sarah Whitlam. She was his first real love, and Nicol 'courted her for a week and upwards, and would have married her on the spot had there been a clergyman on board'. She was, he said, 'as kind and true a creature as ever lived'. Before the voyage was out she bore him a son, John.

On the evening of 3 June 1790 the *Lady Juliana*

---

1 Flynn, Michael, *The Second Fleet: Britain's Grim Convict Armada of 1790*, Library of Australian History, Sydney, 1993, 1–8.

entered Port Jackson after almost a year at sea. Nicol records how the landing was 'almost to our sorrow'. He knew his time with Sarah was running out. But it was a special moment, for that evening John Nicol and Watkin Tench—the great chronicler of the birth of European Australia, who had rowed out to meet the ship amid squalls and cloudbursts—stood together under the one set of sails. For Tench the arrival of the *Lady Juliana* was a moment of exquisite joy. 'News burst upon us like meridian splendour on a blind man,' he records as he learned for the first time of the French Revolution, the madness of George III and the loss of the *Guardian* supply ship. Nicol, characteristically, gives us a glimpse of an intensely human story inside this great historic moment. He doesn't care about revolutions, kings or shipwrecks. His thoughts are all about his imminent separation from his new family.

Nicol spent six weeks in Port Jackson with his beloved Sarah and their infant son. They were, perhaps, the happiest days of his life. Although his recollections of Port Jackson were thirty years old by the time they were written down, they are remarkably accurate. He records, for instance that there were only two 'natives' in the town at that time. They were Abaroo and Nanbaree, survivors of the smallpox epidemic who were then living with Surgeon White (Nanbaree) and the Reverend and Mrs Johnson (Abaroo). He also records some curious attributes of the 'sweet tea' which was drunk with such avidity by the first fleeters. Nicol wrote that 'it is infused and drank like the China tea. I liked it much. It requires no sugar and is both a bitter and a sweet'. He also regarded its medicinal qualities highly:

> There was an old female convict, her hair quite grey with age, her face shrivelled, who was suckling a child she had borne in the colony. Everyone went to see her, and I among the rest. It was a strange sight. Her hair was quite white. Her fecundity was ascribed to the sweet tea.

Tench and others tell us of this woman, but none do so with the descriptive vividness of Nicol. And none ascribe her fecundity to the tea!

As the hour of his departure approached, Nicol became desperate to stay with his wife and child. He was, however, contracted to return to England and the ship was short of hands. He relates that:

> It was not without the aid of the military we were brought on board. I offered to lose my wages but we were short of hands ... The captain could not spare a man and requested the aid of the governor. I thus was forced to leave Sarah, but we exchanged faith. She promised to remain true.

Nicol spent the next few years trying to return to Port Jackson, but without success. While thus engaged, he heard from a runaway convict that Sarah had left the colony for Bombay. Nicol did not know what to make of this information, and nor do I. Sarah did not sail for Bombay until 1796, yet Nicol claims to have heard of it in 1791-92.[1] Was Sarah sending out misinformation, or had Nicol misremembered? Given his subsequent sailing schedule, the latter seems unlikely, for after 1794 Nicol was fighting in the French Revolutionary wars. Nicol visited Sarah's parents in Lincoln, but they could tell him nothing. Hoping for the best yet fearing betrayal, he tried to get a passage to Bombay, but could not find a berth, even as a paying passenger. In all his subsequent journeying, the possibility of being reunited with Sarah is continually on his mind. 'She was,' he says, 'still the idol of all my affections.'

In 1801 Nicol returned to his native Edinburgh, being 'too old to undertake any more love pilgrimages after an individual, as I knew not in what quarter of the globe she was, or whether she were dead or alive'. But what of Sarah and her son? The children of convicts were often removed from their parents, and little John's fate is not recorded. Sarah, in contrast, first appears in the records of the colony the day after Nicol's tearful departure, but the telling of that story must await its proper place.

Nicol's Australian interlude occupied a fraction of his twenty-five years at sea. Much of what he records elsewhere is of great interest to the contemporary reader, for he recalls events and cultures which were glossed over by his better educated and better

1 *The Second Fleet*, 461.

connected contemporaries. The importance of Nicol's work is magnified by the fact that he was far above the ordinary in his humanity, memory and wit. He also loved a song, and nowhere does this shine through more clearly than during his visit to Jamaica, where he lived for some time among slaves. He says of these poor people, 'I esteemed them in my heart' and they clearly reciprocated.

Nicol records that during his stay, he and the other crew were fed on a 'cut and come again' basis, and he always ensured that he took a little something extra to give to the plantation slaves. They in return invited him to a dance. Nicol was touched to find that these poorest of the poor had purchased some 'three bit maubi' as they called rum. They did not drink this luxury themselves, but bought it on his account, having heard that sailors prefer it. The vibrancy of the songs he heard that night shone on undimmed in Nicol's memory for over three decades:

> I lost my shoe in an old canoe
> > Johnio, come Winum so;
> I lost my boot in a pilot boat,
> > Johnio, come Winum so

and

> My Massa a bad man,
> > My Missis cry honey,
> Is this the damn nigger
> > You buy wi my money?
> > Ting a ring ting, ting a ring ting, tarro

The cruel treatment of the slaves clearly appalled Nicol. He records the beating of a pregnant woman and the part he and a colleague played in terminating it. He talks of a one-legged runaway blacksmith chained to his bench, and a slave forced to wear a barbarous collar of spikes. His anger at these outrages remained, like the songs, unblunted by the years.

Nicol's next voyage was more carefree. His journey in search of discovery and trade aboard the *King George* was to take him to Hawaii just after the murder of James Cook. Indeed, the *King George* was the first ship to arrive in the islands after Cook's discovery of them. Nicol records that:

> Almost every man on board took a native woman for a wife while the vessel remained ... The fattest woman I ever saw in my life our gunner chose for a wife. We were forced to hoist her on board. Her thighs were as thick as my waist. No hammock in the ship would hold her. Many jokes were cracked upon the pair.

He also records the wonderful facility of the Hawaiians to parody the Europeans:

> We had a merry facetious fellow on board called Dickson. He sung pretty well. He squinted and the natives mimicked him. Abenoue, King of Atooi, could cock his eye like Dickson better than any of his subjects. Abenoue called him Billicany, from his often singing 'Rule Britannia' ... Abenoue loved him better than any man in the ship, and always

embraced him every time they met on shore or in the ship, and began to sing, 'Tule Billicany, Billicany tule,' etc.

Then comes Nootka Sound, the Marianas, and finally back to Nicol's beloved Wampoa in China, which he visited three times. How can we believe that Nicol was befriended there by a Chinaman named Tommy Linn, a barber-surgeon who contracted to shave the entire crew of Nicol's ship during the duration of their stay? Nicol was really at home among the Chinese, and he was accepted into their bosom when he saved a child from drowning.

The current was strong and the boy was carried down with rapidity. I leapt into the river and saved him with great difficulty . . . and soon had the pleasure of delivering him to his father who stood on the beach wringing his hands.

I wished to go on board, but the Chinese would have me to his house where I was most kindly received and got my dinner in great style. I like their manner of setting out the table at dinner. All that is to be eaten is placed upon the table at once, and all the liquors at the same time. You have all before you and you may make your choice.

He also records, in a delightful manner, some examples of the lingua franca used between Chinese and European traders. Here were the antecedents of the diverse modern pidgins of Oceania, some of which are now the national languages of Pacific nations:

Tommy Linn the barber ... was a walking newspaper. His first word every morning was, 'Hey, yaw,
what fashion?' and we used the same phrase to him.
One morning he came, and the first thing he said
was, 'Hey, yaw, what fashion? Soldier man's ship
come to Lingcome bar.' We, after a few hours, heard
that a man-of-war frigate had arrived ...

They are much alarmed at the appearance of a
man-of-war ship, and they often say, 'Englishman
too much cruel, too much fight.' There were some
English seamen flogged for mutiny while we lay in
the river. The Chinese wept like children for the
men, saying, 'Hey, yaw, Englishman too much cruel,
too much flog, too much flog.'

Nicol's final service was aboard a series of ships
fighting in the French Revolutionary Wars. Nicol's
ship the *Goliah* participated in the Battle of the Nile,
one of Nelson's three great victories, and one of the
most celebrated naval victories of all time. What is
surprising is the presence of women and the role they
played in the battle. Nicol writes:

The women behaved as well as the men, and got
a present for their bravery from the grand
signior ... I was much indebted to the gunner's
wife who gave her husband and me a drink of wine
every now and then which lessened our fatigue
much. There were some of the women wounded,
and one woman belonging to Leith died of her
wounds and was buried on a small island in the

bay. One woman bore a son in the heat of the action.

What a birth that must have been! After the guns ceased their booming, Nicol records what 'an awful sight it was. The whole bay was covered with dead bodies, mangled, wounded and scorched'. This carnage had been caused when the French war ship *L'Orient* blew up close to Nicol's *Goliah*. Such an event was rare in the naval warfare of the day.

At the termination of his service Nicol returned to Edinburgh, where he married his cousin Margaret. It was probably a match based more on affection and convenience than love. He had saved a relatively large sum (which was apparently kept sewn in his clothes) from his decades at sea, and this enabled him to set up a prosperous cooperage business. He also purchased a small cottage and for a time enjoyed married life. But then war (the Napoleonic Wars) broke out again, and the press gangs began their ghastly rounds. These gangs were sanctioned to kidnap and sell into forced labour any sailor they could find.

It is hard for us, in our egalitarian age, to understand just what a threat the press gangs represented to someone such as Nicol. The most vivid description of their rapacity comes from Admiral Anson's *Voyage Around the World*.[1] Although it was written sixty years

1 Walter, R., *A Voyage Round the World in the Years 1740, 1, 2, 3, 4 by George Anson, Esq.*, Alex Lawrie & Co., Edinburgh, 1741, 1804, 20.

earlier, little had changed by Nicol's time. The various efforts made to obtain marines for Anson all failed until:

> five hundred invalids [were] to be collected from the out pensioners of Chelsea college ... who, from their age, wounds, or other infirmities, are incapable of service in marching regiments ... But instead of five hundred, there came on board no more than two hundred and fifty nine; for all those who had limbs and strength to walk out of Portsmouth, deserted, leaving behind them only such as were literally invalids, most of them being sixty years of age, and some of them upwards of seventy.

This 'aged and diseased detachment' was destined to undertake a five-year-long voyage around the world, which was almost unequalled in its arduousness. They dropped like flies. The wounds some had received over fifty years before broke open afresh due to the scurvy. Few survived to see action, much less their homeland.

And so we find John Nicol, newly married at the age of forty-six, unable to sleep in his own bed for fear of being pressed. For eleven years he was forced to live the life of a fugitive in rural Scotland. Yet he remained loyal to king and country, and upon hearing the news of the victory at Trafalgar recalled:

> None but an old tar can feel the joy I felt. I wrought none the next day but walked about enjoying the feeling of triumph. Every now and then I felt the greatest desire to hurra aloud, and many an hurra my heart gave that my mouth uttered not.

To 'hurra' of course, would have alerted the press gangs to his being 'an old tar'.

Finally, at the age of fifty-eight, Nicol felt that it was safe to return home. His homecoming was a joyous one. Perhaps the excitement was too much for Margaret, his wife, for she did not long outlive it. Her death brought on another trial, for Nicol discovered that for years there had been 'more money going out than I by my industry could bring in ... and a number of debits ... had been contracted unknown to me'.

Nicol travelled to London in search of the pension he desperately needed and richly deserved. His fate in this endeavour would be familiar to anyone who has been shunted from one part of the bureaucracy to another. First he learned that his old friend Captain Portlock, who could have provided a testimonial of his service, had died six weeks earlier. He then went to Somerset House to gain a certificate of service. A clerk there sent him to Admiralty House where another clerk told him he had waited too long before applying. As a last ditch effort to gain the all-important certificate he went to see the governor of Greenwich Hospital, but he was on holiday in Scotland. Broke, Nicol returned to Edinburgh.

And so, in the early spring of 1822, at the age of sixty-seven, this fine old sailor was forced to walk the streets of his city, seeking fragments of coal to prevent himself from dying of cold. Had he not met John Howell he would have died in anonymity.

It is heartwarming to know that Howell's charity

really did make a difference to Nicol, for unlike so many of his fellows, he 'died like an admiral, in bed, having evenly rounded out his threescore years and ten'.[1] His funds were not exhausted even then, for a sum of 30 pounds was left to his relatives.

As great as Howell's gift was to Nicol, he left the world a far greater one, for Nicol's recollections offer a unique glimpse of an extraordinary world as it was seen through the eyes of a simple yet most acute watcher upon life. Nicol's tale still has the power to inspire us to adventure, and surely his prayers still go with those who love travel:

> Old as I am, my heart is still unchanged; and were I young and stout as I have been, again would I sail upon discovery—but, weak and stiff, I can only send my prayers with the tight ship and her merry hearts.

*

I have used the text of the original edition of *The Life and Adventures of John Nicol, Mariner*, published by William Blackwood in Edinburgh in 1822. I have modernised Nicol's spelling and punctuation, corrected the occasional error and added some footnotes, marked by an asterisk (*). Nicol's own notes are marked by a dagger (†).

1 *Life and Adventures*, 1937, 25.

A Most Interesting Character

by John Howell

EARLY IN THE spring of the year 1822 John Nicol, the narrator of these adventures, was pointed out to me as a most interesting character, and one who had seen more of the world than most persons in Edinburgh, perhaps in Britain.

He was walking feebly along with an old apron tied round his waist, in which he carried a few very small pieces of coal he had picked up in his wanderings through the streets. From the history I had got of his adventures, I felt grieved to see the poor old man. I requested him to call at my shop. He came in the evening. After a little conversation with him I was astonished at the information he possessed, and the spirit that awoke in the old tar.

I had no interest by which to serve myself. Money I had not to give. As the only means of being of permanent use to him, and perhaps of obtaining the pension he is by service entitled to, I thought of taking down a narrative of his life, from his own mouth. This

I have done, as nearly as I could, in his own words.

Even in the midst of all his present wants, he is a contented cheerful old man of sober habits, and bears an excellent character from those people who have employed him in his trade as a cooper. I have conversed with one of his shipmates who was with him in the *Edgar*, *Goliah* and *Ramilies*, who informs me he was as sober and steady a man as ever sailed.

I have never met with one possessed of a more tenacious memory or who gave a more distinct account of any occurrence he had witnessed, of which any gentleman may satisfy himself, as John will wait upon him with pleasure, upon application to the Publisher.

Edinburgh
12th November 1822

1

*Author's Birth—Early Propensities
—He Goes to London—Is
Apprenticed to a Cooper
—Enters the Navy—Smugglers—
Arrives at Quebec.*

Preface

T O THE PUBLIC it must appear strange that
an unlettered individual, at the advanced
age of sixty-seven years, should sit down to give them
a narrative of his life. Imperious circumstances must
plead my excuse. Necessity, even more than the
importunity of well-wishers, at length compels me. I
shall use my humble endeavour to make it as interesting as is in my power, consistent with truth.

My life, for a period of twenty-five years, was a
continued succession of change. Twice I circumnavi-
gated the globe; three times I was in China, twice in
Egypt, and more than once sailed along the whole
landboard of America from Nootka Sound to Cape
Horn. Twice I doubled it—but I will not anticipate
the events I am about to narrate.

Old as I am, my heart is still unchanged; and were
I young and stout as I have been, again would I sail
upon discovery—but, weak and stiff, I can only send
my prayers with the tight ship and her merry hearts.

John Nicol

I WAS BORN in the small village of Currie, about six miles from Edinburgh, in the year 1755. The first wish I ever formed was to wander, and many a search I gave my parents in gratifying my youthful passion.

My mother died in child-bed when I was very young, leaving my father in charge of five children. Two died young and three came to man's estate. My oldest brother died of his wounds in the West Indies, a lieutenant in the navy. My younger brother went to America and I have never heard from him. Those trifling circumstances I would not mention, were I not conscious that the history of the dispersion of my father's family is the parallel of thousands of the families of my father's rank in Scotland.

My father, a cooper to trade, was a man of talent and information, and made it his study to give his children an education suited to their rank in life; but my unsteady propensities did not allow me to make the most of the schooling I got. I had read *Robinson Crusoe* many times over and longed to be at sea. We had been living for some time in Borrowstownness. Every moment I could spare was spent in the boats or about the shore.

When I was about fourteen years of age my father was engaged to go to London to take a small charge in a chemical work. Even now I recollect the transports my young mind felt when my father informed me I was to go to London. I counted the hours and minutes to the moment we sailed on board the

Glasgow and Paisley Packet, Captain Thompson master. There were a sergeant and a number of recruits, a female passenger, my father, brother and self, besides the crew. It was in the month of December we sailed, and the weather was very bad. All the passengers were seasick; I never was.

This was in the year 1769, when the dreadful loss was sustained on the coast of Yorkshire—above thirty sail of merchantmen were wrecked. We were taken in the same gale but rode it out. Next morning we could hardly proceed for wreck, and the whole beach was covered. The country people were collecting and driving away the dead bodies in wagons.

My father embraced this opportunity to prejudice me against being a sailor. He was a kind but strict parent and we dared not disobey him. The storm had made no impression upon my mind sufficient to alter my determination. My youthful mind could not separate the life of a sailor from dangers and storms, and I looked upon them as an interesting part of the adventures I panted after. I had been on deck all the time and was fully occupied in planning the means of escape. I enjoyed the voyage much, was anxious to learn everything, and was a great favourite with the captain and crew.

One of my father's masters was translating a French work on chemistry. I went to the printing office with the proofs almost every day. Once, in passing near the Tower, I saw a dead monkey floating in the river. I had not seen above two or three in my life. I thought it of great value.

I stripped at once and swam in for it. An English boy, who wished it likewise but who either would or could not swim, seized it when I landed, saying 'he would fight me for it'. We were much of a size. Had there been a greater difference, I was not of a temper to be easily wronged—so I gave him battle. A crowd gathered and formed a ring. Stranger as I was, I got fair play. After a severe contest, I came off victor. The English boy shook hands, and said, 'Scotchman, you have won it.'

I had fought naked as I came out of the water, so I put on my clothes and carried off the prize in triumph—came home and got a beating from my father for fighting and staying my message; but the monkey's skin repaid me for all my vexations.

I remained in London scarcely twelve months when my father sent me to Scotland to learn my trade. I chose the profession of a cooper to please my father. I was for some time with a friend at the Queensferry but, not agreeing with him, I served out my tedious term of apprenticeship at Borrowstownness. My heart was never with the business. While my hands were hooping barrels my mind was at sea and my imagination in foreign climes.

Soon as my period of bondage expired I bade my friends farewell and set out to Leith with a merry heart; and, after working journeyman a few months, to enable me to be a proficient in my trade, I entered on board the *Kent's Regard*, commanded by Lieutenant Ralph Dundas. She was the tender at this time (1776) stationed in Leith Roads.

Now I was happy, for I was at sea. To me the order to weigh anchor and sail for the Nore was the sound of joy.* My spirits were up at the near prospect of obtaining the pleasures I had sighed for since the first dawn of reason. To others it was the sound of woe, the order that cut off the last faint hope of escape from a fate they had been impressed into much against their inclination and interest. I was surprised to see so few who, like myself, had chosen it for the love of that line of life. Some had been forced into it by their own irregular conduct but the greater number were impressed men.**

Ogilvie's revenue cutter and the *Hazard* sloop of war had a short time before surprised a smuggling cutter delivering her cargo in St Andrew's Bay. The smuggler fought them both until all her ammunition was spent, and resisted their boarding her until the very last by every means in their power. A good many of the king's men were wounded, and not a few of the smugglers. When taken possession of they declared the captain had been killed in the action and thrown overboard. The remainder were marched to Edinburgh Castle and kept there until the evening before

* The Nore: a lighthouse near Hastings on the south-east coast of England.
** These were men who had been kidnapped by press gangs and forced into naval service.

we sailed. When they came on board we were all struck with their stout appearance and desperate looks; a set of more resolute fellows I have never in my life met with. They were all sent down to the press-room. The volunteers were allowed to walk the decks and had the freedom of the ship.

One night, on our voyage to the Nore, the whole ship was alarmed by loud cries of murder from the press-room. An armed force was sent down to know the cause and quell the riot. They arrived just in time to rescue, with barely the life, from the hands of these desperadoes, a luckless wretch who had been an informer for a long time in Leith. A good many in the press-room were indebted to him for their present situation.

The smugglers had learned from them what he was and with one accord had fallen upon him and beat him in a dreadful manner. When he was brought to the surgeon's berth there were a number of severe cuts upon his person. From his disgraceful occupation of informer, few on board pitied him. After a few days he got better and was able to walk, but was no more sent down to the press-room.

Upon our arrival at the Nore, a writ of *habeas corpus* was sent on board for one of the smugglers for a debt. We all suspected him to have been the captain, and this a scheme to get him off from being kept on board of a man of war.

I was sent on board the *Proteus*, twenty-gun ship, commanded by Captain Robinson, bound for New

York.* The greater number of the smugglers were put on board the same vessel. They were so stout, active, and experienced seamen that Captain Robinson manned his barge with them.

We sailed from Portsmouth with ordnance stores and 100 men to man the floating batteries upon Lake Champlain.**

I was appointed cooper, which was a great relief to my mind, as I messed with the steward in his room. I was thus away from the crew. I had been much annoyed and rendered very uncomfortable, until now, from the swearing and loose talking of the men in the tender. I had all my life been used to the strictest conversation, prayers night and morning. Now I was in a situation where family worship was unknown and, to add to the disagreeable situation I was in, the troops were unhealthy. We threw overboard every morning a soldier or a sheep.

At first I said my prayers and read my Bible in private, but truth makes me confess I gradually became more and more remiss, and before long I was a sailor like the rest; but my mind felt very uneasy and I made many weak attempts to amend.

We sailed with our convoy direct for Quebec. Upon our arrival the men, having been so long on salt provisions, made too free with the river water and

---

* The American War of Independence had begun.
** Lake Champlain: American Lake bordering New York and Vermont.

were almost all seized with the flux.* The *Proteus* was upon this account laid up for six weeks, during which time the men were in the hospital. After having done the ship's work, Captain Robinson was so kind as allow me to work on shore, where I found employment from a Frenchman who gave me excellent encouragement. I worked on shore all day and slept on board at night.

* The flux: dysentry.

2

Canada—Mode of Fishing—
Serpents—Floats of Wood—Author
Sails to the West Indies—Slavery—
Arrives at Newfoundland.

CANADA IS A fine country. Provisions abound in it and the inhabitants are kind and humane. Salmon abound in the St Lawrence. The Indians come alongside every day with them, either smoked or fresh, which they exchange for biscuit or pork. They take them in wicker baskets wrought upon stakes stuck into the sand within the tide mark. The baskets have two entrances, one pointing up the river, the other pointing down. The entrances have no doors, but sharp-pointed wands prevent the exit of the fish or their returning: if once the head is entered the whole body must follow. They resemble in this the wire mouse trap used in Britain. Some have shutting doors, as in Scotland, that swing with the tide. When it is back, the Indians examine their baskets, and seldom find them without more or less fish.

The French eat many kinds of the serpents that abound in the country. Whether they are good eating I do not know, as I never could bring myself to taste them. They must be good, as it is not for want of other varieties they are made choice of. I often went of an evening with my master to catch them. We caught them with forked sticks; the Frenchman was very dexterous and I soon learned. We often caught two dozen in an evening. When we perceived one we ran the forks of the stick upon its neck, behind the head, and, holding it up from the ground, beat it upon the head with the other until we dispatched it. When we came home the heads were cut off and the snakes skinned. Their skins were very beautiful and many of

the officers got scabbards made of them for their
swords.

I was much surprised at the immense floats of
wood that came gliding majestically down the river
like floating islands. They were covered with turf, and
wood huts upon them, smoke curling from the roofs,
and children playing before the doors and the stately
matron on her seat, sewing or following her domestic
occupations, while the husband sat upon the front
with his long pole, guiding it along the banks or from
any danger in the river, and their batteau astern to
carry them home with the necessaries they procured
by the sale of their wood, the produce of their severe
winter's labour.*

They had floated thus down the majestic St
Lawrence hundreds of miles. It looked like magic and
reminded me of the fairies I had often heard of, to see
the children sporting and singing in chorus upon these
floating masses, the distance diminishing the size of
their figures and softening the melody of their voices,
while their hardy enterprise astonished the mind upon
reflection, and the idea of their enjoyment was dashed
at the recollection of their hardships. They really are
a cheerful race.

I can think of no pleasure more touching to the
feelings and soothing to the mind than to lie upon the
green banks and listen to the melodious voices of the

* Batteau: a light, flat-bottomed river boat used widely in
  Canada.

women of a summer evening as they row along in their batteaux, keeping time to the stroke of the oar. For hours I have lain over the breast-netting, looking and listening to them, unconscious of the lapse of time.

The time I had passed since my entrance into the St Lawrence was very pleasant. In our passage up we had run at an amazing rate—the trees and every object seemed to glide from us with the rapidity of lightning, the wind being fresh and direct. We passed the island of Antecost at a short distance and anchored at the island of Beak where the pilots live. It had an old sergeant, at the time, for governor, Ross his name, who had been with Wolfe at the taking of Quebec.

We then stood up the river, wind and tide serving, and passed next the island of Conder. It appeared a perfect garden. Then the Falls of Morant, the mist rising to the clouds. They appeared to fall from a greater height than the vane of our topmast, and made a dreadful roaring. We last of all made the island of Orleans, a most beautiful place. It is quite near the town and is, like the island of Conder, a perfect garden from end to end.

At length our men were all recovered and the stores landed. I bade farewell to my French master and friends on shore, and sailed for Gaspé Bay. We were joined here by the *Assistance*, fifty-gun ship, commanded by Captain Worth.

All the crew got a handsome treat from Governor O'Hara at the baptism of his family. They were beautiful children, five in number, the oldest a stately girl. None of them had yet been baptised, and the governor embraced the opportunity of the chaplain of the *Assistance* to have this necessary Christian rite performed, as there was not a clergyman at the station and the children had all been born in the Bay. The contrast between the situation of these children and their parents, and the people in Scotland, at the time, made a deep impression upon my mind; and I can say, at no period of my life had the privileges I had left behind appeared so valuable.

From Gaspe Bay we sailed with convoy for the West Indies. The convoy was loaded with salt fish. The American privateers swarmed around like sharks, watching an opportunity to seize any slow-sailing vessel. We took a few of them and brought the convoy safe to its destination.

While watering at St Kitt's we got free of the smugglers. The manner of their escape is the best comment upon their character. Captain Robinson went ashore in his barge. The crew, as I said before, was composed of them, coxswain and all. Soon after the captain left the water's edge they took to their heels. One of them became faint-hearted after he was away and returned. The others, that very night, while search was making for them, seized a boat belonging to the island and rowed over to St Eustatia, a Dutch neutral island, boarded, overpowered and carried off an American brig, and sold her at one of the French islands. None of them were ever taken that I heard of. The one that returned never again held up his head, as he was looked down upon by the crew.

While we lay at any of the West Indian islands our decks used to be crowded by the female slaves, who brought us fruit and remained on board all Sunday until Monday morning—poor things! And all to obtain a bellyful of victuals. On Monday morning the Jolly Jumper, as we called him, was on board with his whip; and, if all were not gone, did not spare it upon their backs.

One cruel rascal was flogging one on our deck, who was not very well in her health. He had struck her once as if she had been a post. The poor creature gave a shriek. Some of our men, I knew not which— there were a good many near him—knocked him overboard. He sunk like a stone. The men gave a hurra! One of the female slaves leaped from the boat alongside into the water and saved the tyrant, who, I have no doubt, often enough beat her cruelly.

I was one of the boarders. We were all armed, when required, with a pike to defend our own vessel should the enemy attempt to board; a tomahawk, cutlass and brace of pistols to use in boarding them. I never had occasion to try their use on board the *Proteus*, as the privateers used to strike after a broadside or two.

While we lay at St Kitt's I took the country fever and was carried to the hospital, where I lay for some days; but my youth, and the kindness of my black nurse, triumphed over the terrible malady. When able to crawl about the hospital, where many came in sick the one day and were carried out the next to be buried, the thoughts of the neglect of my Maker, and the difference in the life I had for some time led from the manner in which I had been trained up in my youth, made me shudder. With tears I promised myself to reform.

I could now see the land-crabs running through the graves of two or three whom I had left stout and full of health. In the West Indies the grave is dug no deeper than just to hold the body, the earth covering it only a few inches, and all is soon consumed by the land-crabs. The black fellows eat them. When I asked them why they eat these loathsome creatures their answer was, 'Why, they eat me.'

I returned on board free from the fever, but very weak. Soon after we took convoy for England, then sailed into Portsmouth harbour and were docked and repaired. While my weakness lasted, my serious impressions remained, but I must again confess: as I became strong in my body, the impressions upon my mind became weak.

As soon as the *Proteus* was repaired we took convoy for St John's, Newfoundland. On this voyage we had very severe weather. Our foremast was carried away and we arrived off St John's in a shattered state, weary and spent with fatigue. To add to our misfortunes we were three weeks lying before the harbour, and could not make it, on account of an island of ice that blocked up its mouth. During these three tedious weeks we never saw the sun or sky, the fogs were so dense. Had it not been for the incessant blowing of the fishermen's horns to warn each other, and prevent their being run down, we might as well have been in the middle of the ocean in a winter night. The bows of the *Proteus* could not be seen from her quarter-deck. We received supplies and intelligence from the harbour by the fishermen. At length this tedious fog cleared up, and we entered the harbour. The *Proteus*, having been an old East India-man, was now quite unfit for service; and the admiral caused her be made a prison-ship.

After this I was wholly employed on shore, brewing spruce for the fleet.* I had two and often three men under me to cut the spruce and firewood for my use. I was a man of some consequence even with the inhabitants, as I could make a present of a bottle of essence to them. They made presents of rum to me. I thus lived very happy, and on good terms with them.

Nothing surprised me more than the early marriage of the Newfoundland females. They have children at twelve years of age. I had some dealings with a merchant, and dined two or three times at his house. I inquired at him for his daughter, a pretty young woman whom I saw at table the first time. To my astonishment he told me she was his wife and the mother of three fine children.

* Spruce: a kind of beer made from spruce (*Picea*) and sugar, and slightly fermented.

In the winter, the cold on the Barrens, as the inhabitants call them, is dreadful. The Barrens are the spaces where there is no wood. Over these we must use our utmost speed to reach the woods. When once there, we are in comparative comfort; it is even warm among the trees. The thoughts of the Barrens again to be crossed is the only damp to our present enjoyment, as we are soon in a sweat from the exercise in cutting the wood.

When the snow first sets in it is necessary to remain at home until the weather clears up. Then the men put on their snow shoes, and three or four abreast thus make a path to the woods. In the middle of the day the sun hardens the path, and along these the wood is dragged upon sledges to the town by dogs. A person, not knowing the cause, would smile to see us urging on our dogs, ourselves pulling with one hand and rubbing our ears with the other. I am certain it would be a cure for tardiness of any kind to be forced to cross the Barrens in winter.

Numbers of the fishermen, who have gambled away their hard-won summer's wages, are forced thus to earn their winter's maintenance. At this time the greater part of the fishers were Irishmen, the wildest characters man can conceive. Gambling and every vice was familiar to them. Their quarrelling and fighting never ceased, and even murders were sometimes perpetrated upon each other. St Patrick's day is a scene of riot and debauchery unequalled in any town in Ireland.

I saw them myself march in line past an unfortunate man who had been killed in one of their feuds, and each man that passed him gave the inanimate body a blow, at the same time calling him by a term of abuse, significant of the party he had belonged to. It was unsafe to carry anything after nightfall. I have been attacked and forced to fight my way more than once. The respectable inhabitants are thus kept under a sort of bondage to this riotous race.

In the summer I was much annoyed by the mosquitos and yellow nippers, a worse fly; for they bite cruelly. They make such a buzzing and noise at night I could not close an eye without my mosquito dose, that is, rum and spruce.

3

Action between the Surprise *and*
Jason—*Anecdotes*—*Miscellaneous*
Occurrences—*Punishment for*
Neglect of Orders—*Author Paid Off.*

I HAD NOW been eighteen months on shore when I was ordered by Admiral Montague on board the *Surprise*, twenty-eight-gun frigate, commanded by Captain Reeves. Her cooper had been killed a few days before in a severe action with an American vessel.

On board the *Surprise* we had a rougher crew than in the *Proteus*; ninety of them were Irishmen, the rest from Scotland and England. We kept cruising about, taking numbers of the America privateers. After a short but severe action we took the *Jason* of Boston, commanded by the famous Captain Manly, who had been commodore in the American service, had been taken prisoner and broke his parole. When Captain Reeves hailed and ordered him to strike, he returned for answer, 'Fire away! I have as many guns as you.' He had heavier metal but fewer men than the *Surprise*. He fought us for a long time.

I was serving powder as busy as I could, the shot and splinters flying in all directions, when I heard the Irishmen call from one of the guns (they fought like devils, and the captain was fond of them on that account), 'Halloo, Bungs, where are you?'*

I looked to their gun and saw the two horns of my study† across its mouth. The next moment it was through the *Jason's* side. The rogues thus disposed of my study, which I had been using just before the

* Bungs: slang name for a cooper.
† anvil.

action commenced and had placed in a secure place, as I thought, out of their reach. 'Bungs for ever!' they shouted when they saw the dreadful hole it made in the *Jason's* side. Bungs was the name they always gave the cooper.

When Captain Manly came on board the *Surprise* to deliver his sword to Captain Reeves, the half of the rim of his hat was shot off. Our captain returned his sword to him again, saying, 'You have had a narrow escape, Manly.'

'I wish to God it had been my head,' he replied.

When we boarded the *Jason*, we found thirty-one cavalry, who had served under General Burgoyne, acting now as marines on board the *Jason*.

A marine of the name of Kennedy, belonging to the *Surprise*, an intelligent lad and well-behaved, was a great favourite with the surgeon. They used to be constantly together reading and acquiring information. They came from the same place, had been at school together and were dear friends. Kennedy's relations were in a respectable line of life. I never learned the cause of his filling his present lowly situation. As it fell out, poor Kennedy was placed sentinel over the spirit-room of the *Jason*. He was, as I have said, an easy kind of lad and had not been long from home.

He allowed the men to carry away the spirits and they were getting fast drunk when the prize-master perceived it. Kennedy was relieved and sent on board the *Surprise*, and next morning put in irons on board the *Europa*, the admiral's ship, where he was tried by a court-martial and sentenced to be hanged on the fore-yardarm.

His offence, no doubt, was great, for the men would all have been so much the worse of liquor in a short time that the Americans could have recovered the *Jason* with ease. Yet we were all sorry for him, and would have done anything in our power to redeem him from his present melancholy situation. His friend the surgeon was inconsolable and did everything in his power. He drew up a petition to the admiral for pardon, stating his former good behaviour, his youth and good connections, and everything he could think of in his favour—but all would not do.

He was taken to the place of execution, the rope round his neck. The match was lit, the clergyman at his post. We were all aloft and upon deck to see him run up to the yardarm amidst the smoke of the gun, the signal of death.

When everyone looked for the command to fire, the admiral was pleased to pardon him. He was sent on board the *Surprise* more like a corpse than a living man. He could scarce walk and seemed indifferent to everything on board, as if he knew not whether he was dead or alive. He continued thus for a long time, scarce speaking to anyone. He was free and did no duty, and was the same on board as a passenger.

When the *Surprise* was in port Captain Reeves allowed a degree of licence to his men, but was a strict disciplinarian at sea, punishing the smallest fault. As

we lay in the harbour after the capture of Captain
Manly we got some prize money, and the crew were
very merry. I, as cooper, was down in the steward's
berth. (It was my duty as cooper to serve out the water
and provisions at the regular times.) All my duty at
the time was over and I was in my berth along with
the steward, enjoying ourselves, when a noise and
tumult on board roused us.

We were not touched with liquor; drunkenness was
a vice I never was addicted to. We came upon deck.
The crew were all fighting through amongst each
other in their drink, English against Irish, the officers
mostly on shore, and those on board looking on. I
meant to take no share in the quarrel, when an Irishman came staggering up, crying, 'Erin go bragh!' and
made a blow at me.

My Scottish blood rose in a moment at this prov-
ocation and I was as throng as the rest. How it ended
I hardly recollect. I got a blow that stupefied me, and
all was quiet when I came to myself, the liquor having
evaporated from the others, and the passion from me.

Soon after this we hailed an American privateer
commanded by a Captain Revel, and she struck. He
was a different character from the gallant Manly. The
weather was so foul and the sea ran so high, we could
not send our boat on board, neither could theirs come
on board of us. Captain Reeves ordered her under our
quarter. As he sailed alongside, the weather still very
stormy and night coming on, we were hailed by voices
calling to us, scarcely to be distinguished in the

rattling of our rigging and the howling of the blast. At length we made out with difficulty, that the American captain was going to make some prisoners he had walk overboard.

Captain Reeves, in great anger, ordered the privateer to place a light on her maintop—instead of which he placed one on a float and cast it adrift. The voices again hailed and let us know what had been done. Captain Reeves called to the American that he would sink her in a moment if he did not do as desired and come close under our lee. Towards morning the weather moderated, and we brought Revel and his prisoners on board the *Surprise*. He was a coarse, ill-looking fellow. His treatment of the prisoners made his own treatment the worse: while Manly dined every day at the captain's table, Revel messed by himself or where he chose with the prisoners.

We took convoy for Lisbon, thence to England where we brought Manly and Revel to be detained during the war in Mill Prison. Revel made his escape from the sergeant of marines on his way to the prison, for which the sergeant was tried by a court-martial and sentenced to be hanged, but was afterwards pardoned. It was nothing uncommon for us to take the same men prisoners once or twice in the same season.

We again took convoy for St John's. In the fleet was a vessel called the *Ark* commanded by Captain Noah. She was an armed transport. This we called *Noah's Ark*. In our voyage out an American privateer, equal in weight of metal but having forty-five men (the *Ark* only sixteen), bore down upon her. The gallant Noah, in his *Ark*, gave battle, we looking on, and after a sharp contest took the American and brought her alongside, her captain lying dead upon her deck. Captain Reeves, with consent of the crew, gave the prize to Noah, who carried her in triumph to Halifax and sold her.

One of our men was whipped through the fleet for stealing some dollars from a merchant ship he was assisting to bring into port. It was a dreadful sight: the unfortunate sufferer tied down on the boat and rowed from ship to ship, getting an equal number of lashes at the side of each vessel from a fresh man. The poor wretch, to deaden his sufferings, had drunk a whole bottle of rum a little before the time of punishment. When he had only two portions to get of his punishment, the captain of the ship perceived he was tipsy and immediately ordered the rest of the punishment to be delayed until he was sober. He was rowed back to the *Surprise*, his back swelled like a pillow, black and blue. Some sheets of thick blue paper were steeped in vinegar and laid to his back. Before he seemed insensible. Now his shrieks rent the air. When better he was sent to the ship, where his tortures were stopped and again renewed.

During the remainder of the war, our duty was the same, taking convoy and capturing American privateers. We came to England with convoy and were docked, then had a cruise in the Channel where we took the *Duke de Chartres*, eighteen-gun ship, and were ourselves chased into Monts Bay on the coast of Cornwall by a French sixty-four. We ran close inshore and were covered by the old fort which, I believe, had not fired a ball since before the time of Oliver Cromwell—but it did its duty nobly, all night the Frenchman keeping up his fire, the fort and *Surprise* returning it. When day dawned he sheered off, and we only suffered a little in our rigging. The only blood that was shed on our side was an old fogie of the fort who was shot by his own gun.

Quite weary of the monotonous convoy duty and having seen all I could see, I often sighed for the verdant banks of the Forth. At length my wishes were gratified by the return of peace. The *Surprise* was paid off in the month of March 1783. When Captain Reeves came ashore, he completely loaded the long-boat with flags he had taken from the enemy. When one of the officers inquired what he would do with them, he said, laughing, 'I will hang one upon every tree in my father's garden.'

4

Author Arrives in Scotland—
Singular Adventure—He Returns to
London—Enters a Greenland Ship—
Whale Fishery.

I NO SOONER had the money that was due me in my hat than I set off for London direct and, after a few days of enjoyment, put my bedding and chest on board a vessel bound for Leith. Every halfpenny I had saved was in it but nine guineas, which I kept upon my person to provide for squalls. The trader fell down the river but, there being no wind and the tide failing, the captain told us we might sleep in London, only to be sure to be on board before eight o'clock in the morning. I embraced the opportunity and lost my passage.

As all my savings were in my chest, and a number of passengers on board whom I did not like, I immediately took the diligence to Newcastle.* There were no mails running direct for Edinburgh every day, as now. It was the month of March, yet there was a great deal of snow on the ground; the weather was severe, but not so cold as at St John's.

When the diligence set off there were four passengers: two ladies, another sailor and myself. Our lady companions, for the first few stages, were proud and distant, scarcely taking any notice of us. I was restrained by their manner. My companion was quite at home chatting to them, unmindful of their monosyllabic answers. He had a good voice and sung snatches of sea songs, and was unceasing in his endeavours to please. By degrees their reserve wore off and the conversation became general. I now

* Diligence: public stage coach.

learned they were sisters who had been on a visit to a
relation in London and were now returning to their
father, who was a wealthy farmer.

Before it grew dark we were all as intimate as if
we had sailed for years in the same ship. The oldest,
who appeared to be about twenty, attached herself to
me and listened to my accounts of the different places
I had been in with great interest. The youngest was
as much interested by my volatile companion.

I felt a something uncommon arise in my breast as
we sat side by side. I could think of nothing but my
pretty companion. My attentions were not disagreeable to her and I began to think of settling, and how
happy I might be with such a wife.

After a number of efforts I summoned resolution
to take her hand in mine. I pressed it gently. She drew
it faintly back. I sighed. She laid her hand upon my
arm, and in a whisper inquired if I was unwell. I was
upon the point of telling her what I felt, and my
wishes, when the diligence stopped at the inn.

I wished we had been sailing in the middle of the
Atlantic, for a covered cart drove up and a stout hearty
old man welcomed them by their names, bestowing a
hearty kiss upon each. I felt quite disappointed. He
was their father. My pretty Mary did not seem to be
so rejoiced at her father's kind salutation as might
have been expected.

My companion, who was an Englishman, told me
he would proceed no farther, but endeavour to win
the hand of his pretty partner. I told him my present

situation, that my chest and all I had was on board the Leith trader, and no direction upon it. On this account I was forced to proceed as fast as possible or I would have remained and shared his fortunes with all my heart. I took leave of them with a heavy heart, resolving to return. I could perceive Mary turn pale as I bade her farewell, while her sister looked joy itself when Williams told them he was to proceed no farther. Before the coach set off, I made him promise to write me an account of his success, and that I would return as soon as I had secured my chest and seen my father. He promised to do this faithfully.

I whispered Mary a promise to see her soon, and pressed her hand as we parted. She returned the pressure. I did not feel without hope. When the farmer drove off, Williams accompanying them, I only wished myself in his place.

When the coach reached Newcastle, I soon procured another conveyance to Edinburgh and was at Leith before the vessel. When she arrived I went on board and found all safe. I then went to Borrowstownness, but found my father had been dead for some time.

This was a great disappointment and grief to me. I wished I had been at home to have received his last blessing and advice, but there was no help. He died full of years; and that I may be as well prepared when I shall be called hence is my earnest wish. After visiting his grave and spending a few days with my friends, I became uneasy at not hearing from

Williams. I waited for three weeks; then, losing all patience, I set off myself to see how the land lay. I took leave of home once more, with a good deal of money in my pocket, as I had been almost a miser at home, keeping all for the marriage, should I succeed.

The spring was now advancing apace, when I took my passage in a Newcastle trader and arrived safe at the inn where I had last parted from Mary. It was night when I arrived and, being weary, soon went to bed. I was up betimes in the morning. When I met Williams, he was looking very dull. I shook hands, and asked, 'What cheer?'

He shook his head, and said, 'Why, Jack, we are on the wrong tack, and I fear will never make port. I had no good news to send, so it was of no use to write. I was at the farmer's last night. He swears, if ever I come near his house again, he will have me before the justice as an idle vagrant. My fair jilt is not much concerned, and I can scarce get a sight of her. She seems to shun me.'

I felt a chillness come over me at this information, and asked him what he meant to do.

'Why, set sail this day. Go to my mother, give her what I can spare, and then to sea again. My store is getting low here. But what do you intend to do, Jack?'

'Truth, Williams, I scarce know. I will make one trip to the farm, and if Mary is not as kind as I hope to find her I will be off too.'

Soon after breakfast I set off for the farmer's with an anxious heart. On my arrival I met Mary in the yard. She seemed fluttered at sight of me but, sum-moning up courage as I approached, she made a distant bow and coldly asked me how I did. I now saw there was no hope and had not recovered myself when her father came out, and in a rough manner demanded what I wanted and who I was. This in a moment brought me to myself and, raising my head, which had been bent towards the ground, I looked at him.

Mary shrunk from my gaze but the old man came close up to me, and again demanded what I wanted.

'It is of no consequence,' I answered. Then, looking at Mary, 'I believe I am an unwelcome visitor—it is what I did not expect—so I will not obtrude myself upon you any longer.' I then walked off as indifferent to appearance as I could make myself, but was tempted to look over my shoulder more than once. I saw Mary in tears and her father in earnest conversation with her.

I made up my mind to remain at the inn the rest of that day and all night, in hopes of receiving an appointment to meet Mary. I was loath to think I was indifferent to her—and the feeling of being slighted is so bitter I could have quarrelled with myself and all the world. I sat with Williams at the window all day. No message came. In the morning we bade adieu to the fair jilts with heavy hearts—Williams for his mother's and I for London.

After working a few weeks in London at my own business, my wandering propensities came as strong upon me as ever, and I resolved to embrace the first opportunity to gratify it, no matter whither, only let me wander. I had been many times on the different wharfs looking for a vessel, but the seamen were so plenty there was great difficulty in getting a berth.

I met by accident Captain Bond, who hailed me and inquired if I wished a berth. He had been captain of a transport in the American war. I had favoured him at St John's. I answered him, 'It was what I was looking after.'

'Then, if you will, come and be cooper of the *Leviathan* Greenland ship. I am captain. You may go to Squire Mellish and say I recommend you for cooper.'

I thanked him for his goodwill, went, and was engaged and on board at work next day.

We sailed in a short time for the coast of Greenland, and touched at Lerwick, where we took on board what men we wanted. In the first of the season we were very unsuccessful, having very stormy weather. I at one time thought our doom was fixed. It blew a dreadful gale and we were for ten days completely fast in the ice. As far as we could see all was ice, and the ship was so pressed by it everyone thought we must either be crushed to pieces or forced out upon the top of the ice, there ever to remain.

At length the wind changed and the weather moderated, and where nothing could be seen but ice, in a short time after, all as far as the eye could reach was open sea. What were our feelings at this change it were vain to attempt a description of—it was a reprieve from death.

The horrors of our situation were far worse than any storm I ever was in. In a storm upon a lea-shore, there, even in all its horrors, there is exertion to keep the mind up, and a hope to weather it. Locked up in ice, all exertion is useless. The power you have to contend with is far too tremendous and unyielding. It, like a powerful magician, binds you in its icy circle, and there you must behold, in all its horrors, your approaching fate, without the power of exertion, while the crashing of the ice and the less loud but more alarming cracking of the vessel serve all to increase the horrors of this dreadful sea-mare.

When the weather moderated we were very successful and filled our ship with four fish.* I did not like the whale-fishing. There is no sight for the eye of the inquisitive after the first glance and no variety to charm the mind. Desolation reigns around: nothing but snow, or bare rocks and ice. The cold is so intense and the weather often so thick. I felt so cheerless that I resolved to bid adieu to the coast of Greenland for ever, and seek to gratify my curiosity in more genial climes.

We arrived safe in the river and proceeded up to our situation. But how strange are the freaks of fate! In the very port of London, as we were hurrying to our station, the tide was ebbing fast when the ship missed stays and yawed round, came right upon the Isle of Dogs, broke her back and filled with water.

* These were bowhead whales.

There was none of us hurt and we lost nothing as
she was insured. I was one of those placed upon her
to estimate the loss sustained amongst the casks, and
was kept constantly on board for a long time.

5

*Voyage to Grenada—Treatment of
the Negroes—Dancing and Songs—
Long-Shorers Chiefly Scots and
Irishmen—Anecdote of a Welshman.*

M Y NEXT VOYAGE was on board the *Cotton Planter* commanded by Captain Young, bound for the island of Grenada. I was very happy under Captain Young. He had been long in the Mediterranean trade where he had lost his health, and every year made a voyage to the West Indies to avoid the English winters. We sailed in the month of October, and arrived safe at St George's, Grenada.

I wrought a great deal on shore and had a number of blacks under me. They are a thoughtless, merry race; in vain their cruel situation and sufferings act upon their buoyant minds. They have snatches of joy that their pale and sickly oppressors never know. It may appear strange, yet it is only in the West Indian islands that the pictures of Arcadia are in a faint manner realised once in the week.

When their cruel situation allows their natural propensities to unfold themselves on the evenings of Saturday and Sabbath, no sound of woe is to be heard in this land of oppression—the sound of the Benji[†] and rattle, intermixed with song, alone is heard. I have seen them dancing and singing of an evening, and their backs sore from the lash of their cruel task-masters. I have lain upon deck of an evening, faint and exhausted from the heat of the day, to enjoy the

† The Benji is made of an old firkin [a small cask] with one end out, covered with shark skin, and beat upon with two pieces of wood. The rattles are made of a calabash shell, and a few small pebbles in it, fixed on a wooden handle; these they shake to the time of the Benji.

cool breeze of evening, and their wild music and song, the shout of mirth and dancing, resounded along the beach and from the valleys. There the negroes bounded in all the spirit of health and happiness while their oppressors could hardly drag their effeminate bodies along, from dissipation or the enervating effects of the climate.

These meetings are made up and agreed upon often long before they arrive. The poor and despised slaves will club their scanty earning for the refreshments and to pay Benji men. Many of them will come miles to be present. The females dress in all their finery for the occasion, and the males are decked with any fragments of dress they can obtain. Many of them are powdered. They all ape the manners of their masters as much as is in their power.

It is amusing to see them meet each other; they have so many congées, set phrases and kind inquiries in which Mama is the person most kindly inquired after.* They are as formal as dancing-masters, and make up to each other in civilities for the contempt heaped upon them by the whites.

The food allowed them by their masters is very poor. Half a salt herring, split down the middle, to each (they call it the one-eyed fish upon this account), horse beans and Indian corn constitute their fare. The Indian corn they must grind for themselves on Saturday after their day's task is done, which in general

---

* Congées: ways of saying hello and goodbye.

is to bring one burden of wood to the estate.

From Saturday until Monday morning they have to rest themselves and cultivate their patch of garden ground. Those who live near seaports prefer going to the mountains and gathering coconuts, plantains and other fruit which they sell. The slaves all bring any little fruit or vegetables they have to spare to market.

The sales by the whites, as well as blacks, are all made on the Sabbath day. The jailor of St George's is vendue-master by right of office, and none dare lift a hammer to sell without his permission.*

Captain Young did not keep his crew upon allowance. We had 'cut and come again' always. I often took a piece of lean beef and a few biscuits with me when I went to the plantation, as a present to the blacks. This the poor creatures would divide among themselves to a single fibre. As I had always been kind to them, they invited me and a few other seamen to one of their entertainments. I went with pleasure, to observe their ways more minutely. Upon my arrival I could hardly keep my gravity at their appearance, yet I esteemed them in my heart.

There was one black who acted as master of the ceremonies, but the Benji man appeared greater than any other individual. They all, before they commenced to dance, made their obeisance to him; the same at the conclusion. The master of ceremonies had an old cocked hat, and no courtier could have

* Vendue-master: auctioneer.

used it with more zeal. Many of the females had cast silk gowns which had belonged to their mistresses, and their heads powdered—but they were tawdry figures, though no lady or gentleman could have been more vain of their appearance or put on more airs.

The kind creatures had, upon our account, subscribed for three-bit maubi.[†] When they dance they accompany the Benji with the voice. Their songs were many of them *extempore*, and made on our ship or ourselves. My small gifts were not forgot. Their choruses are common. Their songs are of the simplest kind, as:

> I lost my shoe in an old canoe,
>   Johnio! come Winum so.
> I lost my boot in a pilot boat,
>   Johnio! come Winum so.

Others are satirical, as:

> My Massa a bad man,
>   My Missis cry honey,
> Is this the damn nigger,
>   You buy wi my money.
>   Ting a ring ting, ting a ring ting, tarro.

---

† Maubi is a drink like ginger-beer they drink among themselves, but as they knew sailors liked stouter drink, they bought rum. The price was one shilling and sixpence the gallon. A bit is equal to sixpence. Rum they call three-bit maubi.

Missis cry nigger man
　Do no work, but eattee;
She boil three eggs in pan,
　And gi the broth to me.
　Ting a ring ting, ting a ring ting, tarro.

With such songs as these they accompany the Benji. I do not recollect to have ever heard them sing a plaintive song, bewailing their cruel fate. This made me wonder much, as I expected they would have had many bewailing their destiny. But joy seems on these occasions their only aim.

The dance went on with spirit. I would have joined with pleasure, but it was beyond my strength after my day's work and the heat of the climate. We parted in good time without the least appearance of intoxication. I never in my life was happier, had more attention paid to me, or was more satisfied with an entertainment.

They have one rhyme they use at work, and adjust their motions to it. They never vary it that I heard.

Work away, body, bo
Work aa, jollaa.

In this manner they beguile the irksomeness of labour, but the capricious driver often interrupts their innocent harmony with the crack of his cart whip. No stranger can witness the cruelty unmoved.

George Innes and I were proceeding through the plantation to inform the master the double moses was on the beach for sugar.† A black driver was flogging a woman big with child. Her cries rent the air, the other slaves declaring by their looks that sympathy they dared not utter. George ran to him and gave him a good beating, and swore he would double the gift if he laid another lash upon her. He had not dared when we returned.

There were two or three slaves upon the estate who, having once run away, had iron collars round their necks with long hooks that projected from them to catch the bushes should they run away again. These they wore night and day. There was a black slave, a cooper with a wooden leg, who had run away more than once. He was now chained to the block at which he wrought.

They are much given to talking and story-telling; the Scripture characters of the Old Testament are quite familiar to them. They talk with astonishment of Samson, Goliath, David, etc. I have seen them hold up their hands in astonishment at the strength of the white Buccaras. I have laughed at their personifications. Hurricane, they cannot conceive what it is. There are planters of the name of Kane on the island. Hurricane, they will say, 'He a strong white Buccara, he come from London.'

There was a black upon the estate who had been on the island of St Kitt's when Rodney defeated the

† The double moses is a large boat for taking on board the sugar casks. There are two, the single and double moses. The single holds only one hogshead, the double more.

French fleet. He had seen the action and was never tired speaking of it, nor his auditors of listening. He always concluded with this remark: 'The French 'tand 'tiff, but the English 'tand far 'tiffer. De all de same as game cock, de die on de 'pot.'

They are apt to steal, but are so very credulous they are easily detected. Captain Young gave a black butcher of the name of Coffee a hog to kill. When the captain went to see it, Coffee said, 'This very fine hog, Massa, but I never see a hog like him in all my life, he have no liver, no light.'*

Captain Young: 'That is strange, Coffee. Let me see in the book.' He took a memorandum book out of his pocket, turned over a few leaves, and looked very earnest. 'I see Coffee go to hell bottom—hog have liver and lights.'

Coffee shook like an aspen leaf, and said, 'O Massa, Coffee no go to hell bottom—hog have liver and lights.'

He restored them and, trembling, awaited his punishment. Captain Young only laughed, and made him a present of them.

I one time went with Captain Young to a planter's, where he was to dine, that I might accompany him back to the ship in the evening, as he was weakly. Upon our arrival I was handed over to a black who was butler and house steward. He had been in England and, as he said, seen London and King

* Light: lung.

George. He was by this become a greater man than by his situation among the other slaves, and was as vain in showing the little he knew as if he had been bred at college, and was perpetually astonishing the other slaves, whom he looked down upon, with the depth of his knowledge and his accounts of London and King George.

No professor could have delivered his opinions and observations with more pomp and dogmatism. One of the blacks inquired at me what kind of people the Welsh were. To enjoy the sport, as one of the crew, William Jones, a Welshman, was in company with me at the time, I referred him to the black oracle who, after considering a moment or two, replied with a smile of satisfaction upon his sooty features, 'The English have ships, the Irish have ships and the Scotch have ships, but Welshmen have no ships—they are like the negro man, they live in the bush.'

The Welshman started to his feet and would have knocked him down had I not prevented. He poured out a volley of oaths upon him.

He heard him with indifference, and his assertion was not the least shaken in the opinion of his hearers by the Welshman's violence—it, like many others of equal truth, was quoted and received as gospel. It was long a byword in the ship: 'Welshman live in the bush like negro man.'

Our cook having left the vessel, we were forced to take a long-shorer in his place. They are a set of idle dissipated seamen who will not work or take a berth.

They loiter along the harbours and get drunk by any means, no matter however base. Home they have none. The weather is so warm, they lie out all night and are content with little victuals. They are in general covered with rags and filth, the victims of idleness and disease. It is nothing uncommon to see their feet and ankles a mass of sores, their feet eaten by the jiggers until they resemble fowls' feet, having no flesh on them. Their minds chilled and totally sunk, death soon closes their career.

The next morning after the new cook came on board, he lay so long the captain's kettle was not boiled, nor the fire kindled. Paddy was quite indifferent when the cabin boy told him Captain Young must have the kettle immediately. He replied, 'Let him send his blasters and blowers here then.' Blasters and blowers was sent about his business immediately, and he cared not a fig.

I must confess the long-shorers are mostly composed of Irish and Scots. The very blacks despise them. They could make a good living by carrying water, as they could get a bit a burden. Many blacks get leave from the overseers to do this, giving them a bit a day, and earn as much as buy their freedom. An overseer may often have a dozen blacks thus employed, and his master not a bit the wiser, and the money his own gain.

We brought to England, as passenger from the island, a planter who was very rich and had a number of slaves. He had been a common seaman on board

of a man-of-war, had deserted and lived on shore concealed until his ship sailed. He afterwards married a
free black woman who kept a punch-house, who died
and left him above three thousand pounds. With this
he had bought a plantation and slaves, and was making
money fast. He brought as much fresh provisions and
preserves on board as would have served ten men out
and out, and was very kind to the men in giving them
liquor and fresh provisions.

6

Voyage of Discovery—Anecdote—
Falkland Islands—Cape Horn—
Owhyee—Atooi—Onehow—Manners
of the Natives.

U PON OUR ARRIVAL in London I learned that my old officer, Lieutenant Portlock, now captain, was going out in the *King George*, as commander, in company with the *Queen Charlotte*, Captain Dixon, upon a voyage of discovery and trade round the world.

This was the very cruise I had long wished for. At once I made myself clean and waited upon Captain Portlock. He was happy to see me, as I was an excellent brewer of spruce-beer, and the very man he wished, but knew not where to have sent for me. I was at once engaged on the most liberal terms as cooper, and went away rejoicing in my good fortune. We had a charter from the South Sea Company and one from the India House, as it was to be a trading voyage for furs as well as discovery. This was in the year 1785.

With a joyful heart I entered on this voyage but, through an unforeseen accident, I had more to do than I engaged for. Our steward went on shore for a few necessary articles just before we sailed. He was a foolish lad, got tipsy, and the money sold him. Having spent it, he was ashamed to come on board again. The wind was fair, and I engaged to fill his place rather than delay the voyage one day, so eager was I upon it.

The first land we made was Santa Cruz in the island of Tenerife, where we stayed ten days getting fruit and provisions; then made the island of Sao Tiago (it belongs to the Portuguese) where we watered and took in fresh provisions. While here we caught a number of fish called bass, very like salmon, which we eat fresh. The island is badly cultivated but abounds in cattle. We exchanged old clothes for sheep, or anything the men wanted.

The Portuguese here are great rogues. I bought two fat sheep from one of them. The bargain was made and I was going to lead away my purchase when he gave a whistle and my sheep scampered off to the fields. The fellow laughed at my surprise. I had a great mind to give him a beating for his trick, and take my clothes from him, but we had strict orders not to quarrel with the people upon any account. At length he made a sign that I might have them again by giving a few more articles. I had no alternative but lose what I had given or submit to his roguery. I gave a sign I would. He gave another whistle and the sheep returned to his side. I secured them before I gave the second price.

With all their roguery they are very careless of their money, more so than any people I ever saw. In walking through the town I have seen kegs full of dollars, without heads, standing in the houses, and the door open without a person in the house to look after them.

Having watered, we run for the Falkland Islands. When we arrived we found two American vessels busy whaling. We hoisted our colours, the Anchor and Hope. The Americans took us for Spaniards and set off in all haste. When we landed we found a great number of geese ready plucked and a large fire burning, so we set to work and roasted as many as served us all, and enjoyed them much.

Next morning the Americans came near in their boats, and found out their mistake. Captain Portlock thanked them for their treat. We then had a busy time killing geese. There are two kinds, the water and upland. The water ones are very pretty, spreckled like a partridge. The penguins were so plenty we were forced to knock them out of our way as we walked along the beach.

The pelicans are plenty and build their nests of clay. They are near each other, like a honey-comb. I was astonished how each bird knew its own nest. They appear to hatch in the same nest until they are forced to change by the accumulation of dung. They are so tame I have stood close by when they arrived with their pouch distended with fish, and fed their young without being in the least disturbed.

We killed a number of hogs. Our doctor broke his double-barrelled gun in dispatching one, and sold it afterwards in China for £42. What was of more value to us was a great many iron hoops and beeswax, the remains of some wreck. We picked up some of the wax but took every inch of the hoops. They were more valuable than gold to us for trading with the natives.

When off Cape Horn we perceived an object floating at a small distance from the ship. Not one of us could make out what it was. All our boats being fast, two men went down into the water and swam to it, and made it fast in the slings. When it came on board it was a cask, but so overgrown with weeds and barnacles the bung-hole could not be discovered. I was set to work to cut into it. To our agreeable surprise it was full of excellent port wine. All the crew got a little of it and Captain Portlock gave us brandy in place of the rest.

We next made Staten Island; the weather was fine, but very cold.* We stood away for latitude 23° where we cruised about for some time in quest of islands laid down in our charts. We could find none, but turtle in great abundance. They were a welcome supply, but we soon tired of them, cook them as we could in every variety.

Not finding the islands, we bore away for the Sandwich Islands.** The first land we made was Owhyee, the island where Captain Cook was killed. The *King George* and *Queen Charlotte* were the first ships which had touched there since that melancholy event. The natives came on board in crowds and were happy to see us. They recognised Portlock and others who had been on the island before, along with Cook. Our decks were soon crowded with hogs, breadfruit, yams and potatoes. Our deck soon resembled shambles—our butcher had fourteen assistants.

I was as busy and fatigued as I could be cutting iron hoops into lengths of eight and nine inches which the

---

* Staten Island lies south of Tierra del Fuego.
** The Hawaiian Islands.

carpenter ground sharp. These were our most valuable commodity in the eyes of the natives. I was stationed down in the hold of the vessel, and the ladders were removed to prevent the natives from coming down to the treasury. The King of Owhyee looked to my occupation with a wistful eye; he thought me the happiest man on board to be among such vast heaps of treasure.

Captain Portlock called to me to place the ladder and allow the king to come down, and give him a good long piece. When the king descended he held up his hands and looked astonishment personified. When I gave him the piece of hoop of twenty inches long he retired a little from below the hatch into the shade, undid his girdle, bent the iron to his body and, adjusting his belt in the greatest haste, concealed it. I suppose he thought I had stole it. I could not but laugh to see the king concealing what he took to be stolen goods.*

We were much in want of oil for our lamps. The sharks abounding, we baited a hook with a piece of salt pork and caught the largest I ever saw in any sea. It was a female, nineteen feet long. It took all hands to hoist her on board; her weight made the vessel heel. When she was cut up we took forty-eight young ones out of her belly, eighteen inches long. We saw them go into her mouth after she was hooked.** The hook

---

* The king was more likely hiding it from his fellow Hawaiians.
** The fish seen apparently entering the mouth were probably not young sharks but remora (suckerfish) which habitually accompany larger marine organisms.

was fixed to a chain attached to our mainbrace, or we never would have kept her. It was evening when she snapped the bait; we hauled the head just above the surface, the swell washing over it. We let her remain thus all night and she was quite dead in the morning. There were in her stomach four hogs, four full-grown turtle, beside the young ones. Her liver, the only part we wanted, filled a tierce.*

Almost every man on board took a native woman for a wife while the vessel remained, the men thinking it an honour, or for their gain, as they got many presents of iron, beads or buttons. The women came on board at night and went on shore in the morning. In the evening they would call for their husbands by name. They often brought their friends to see their husbands, who were well pleased, as they were never allowed to go away empty.

The fattest woman I ever saw in my life our gunner chose for a wife. We were forced to hoist her on board. Her thighs were as thick as my waist. No hammock in the ship would hold her. Many jokes were cracked upon the pair.

They are the worst people to pronounce the English of any I ever was among. Captain Portlock they called *Potipoti*. The nearest approach they could make to my name was *Nittie*, yet they would make the greatest efforts, and look so angry at themselves and vexed at their vain efforts.

* A large cask of varying size.

We had a merry facetious fellow on board called Dickson. He sung pretty well. He squinted and the natives mimicked him. Abenoue, King of Atooi, could cock his eye like Dickson better than any of his subjects.* Abenoue called him Billicany, from his often singing 'Rule Britannia'. Abenoue learned the air and the words as near as he could pronounce them. It was an amusing thing to hear the king and Dickson sing. Abenoue loved him better than any man in the ship, and always embraced him every time they met on shore or in the ship, and began to sing, 'Tule Billicany, Billicany tule,' etc.

We had the chief on board who killed Captain Cook for more than three weeks. He was in bad health, and had a smelling-bottle with a few drops in it which he used to smell at. We filled it for him. There were a good many bayonets in possession of the natives, which they had obtained at the murder of Cook.

We left Owhyee and stood down to Atooi, where we watered and had a feast from Abenoue the King. We took our allowance of brandy on shore and spent a most delightful afternoon, the natives doing all in their power to amuse us. The girls danced, the men made a sham fight, throwing their spears. The women, standing behind, handed the spears to the men the same as in battle, thus keeping up a continued shower of spears. No words can convey an adequate

* Atooi: Kauai.

idea of their dexterity and agility. They thought we were bad with the rheumatism, our movements were so slow compared with their own. The women would sometimes lay us down and chafe and rub us, making moan and saying, 'O Rume! O Rume!' They wrestled, but the stoutest man in our ship could not stand a single throw with the least chance of success.

We next stood for Onehow, of which Abenoue was king as well as Atooi, to get yams.* This island grows them in abundance, and scarce any thing else. They have no wood upon the island but exchange their yams for it to build their canoes. While lying here it came to blow a dreadful gale. We were forced to cut our cables and stand out to sea, and leave sixteen men and boys. It was three weeks before we could return. When we arrived we found them well and hearty. These kind people had lodged them two and two in their houses, gave them plenty of victuals and liberty to ramble over the whole island.

The only man who was in the least alarmed for his safety was an old boatswain. He was in continual fear. The innocent natives could not meet to divert themselves, or even a few talk together, but the old sinner would shake with horror and called to his shipmates, 'Now, they are going to murder us—this is our last night.' He was a perfect annoyance to the others. He scarce ever left the beach but to go to some height to look out for the ships, and after looking till he was

* Onehow: Niihau.

almost blind he would seek out the other men to make his lamentations and annoy them with his fears of the loss of the ships or their being deserted by them.

At length we returned and took them on board, making presents to the king and his kind people for their unlimited hospitality. We now took an affectionate leave of these kind islanders.

As the summer now advanced apace we stood over to Cook's River, where we arrived in 1786, eleven months after we left England.* Upon our arrival a number of Russians came on board of us and made the captain a present of salmon, who in return gave them salt, an article they stood much in need of. One of our men, who spoke the Russian tongue, told them we were upon a voyage of discovery. We did not wish them to know we were trading in furs. We parted from them with mutual civilities.

At the entrance of Cook's River is an immense volcanic mountain which was in action at the time, and continued burning all the time we lay there, pouring down its side a torrent of lava as broad as the Thames. At night the sight was grand but fearful. The natives here had their spears headed with copper but, having no one on board who could speak their language, we had no means of learning where they obtained the copper.

While we lay here it was the heat of summer, yet the ice never melted and the snow was lying very deep

* Cook's River: Cook Inlet, Alaska.

on the heights. What a contrast from the delightful islands we had so lately left.

Our longboat, decked and schooner-rigged, proceeded up the river in hopes of finding an outlet, or inland sea. After proceeding with great difficulty and perseverance, until all hopes of success vanished, they returned. We then bore to the southward to Prince William's Sound to pursue our trade with the Indians. They are quite different from the Sandwich Islanders in appearance and habits. They are not cruel but great thieves.

I was employed on shore brewing spruce all day and slept on board at night. One night the Indians, after starting the beer, carried off all the casks: they were iron-hooped.* All our search was vain; no traces of them were to be discovered. To quarrel with the Indians would have defeated the object of our voyage. At length they were discovered by accident in the most unlikely place, in the following manner.

One of our boats had been on a trading excursion detained so long, we became alarmed for its safety. Captain Portlock sent some of our men armed to the top of a high hill to look out for the boat. To the surprise of the men, they found the staves and ends of the barrels, and some large stones they had used in breaking them to pieces. How great must their labour have been in rolling up the barrels and then in dashing them to pieces. Yet I have no doubt

---

* Starting: spilling.

they thought themselves richly rewarded in obtaining the iron hoops. The men brought back a stave or two with the ship's name branded on them to evidence the truth of their discovery. We then moved the brewing place to the other side of the island, within sight of the ship.

I was much annoyed by the natives for some time while working. They would handle the hoops, and every now and then a piece would vanish. There was only a quarter-master and boy with me. While the natives swarmed around I felt rather uncomfortable. They became more and more bold. The captain, seeing from the deck my disagreeable situation, hailed me to set Neptune, our great Newfoundland dog, upon them, saying he would fear them more than fifty men.

I obeyed with alacrity and hounded Neptune, who enjoyed the sport as much as I, to see the great fellows run, screaming like girls, in all directions. I was soon left to pursue my labour unmolested and whenever they grew troublesome Neptune, without orders, put them to the running and screaming. When one approached, if Neptune was near, he would stretch out his arms, and cry, '*Lally, Neptune*'—that is 'friend' in their language. The Indians here could pronounce every word we spoke almost as well as ourselves. This appeared the more strange after hearing the vain efforts of our friends the Sandwich Islanders.

One Sabbath day all the ship's company, except the captain, two boys and the cook, were on shore amusing themselves. During our absence an immense number of the natives came alongside and took complete possession of the vessel and helped themselves to whatever took their fancy. The captain, boys, and cook barricadoed themselves in the cabin and loaded all the muskets and pistols within their reach. Their situation was one of great danger.

The surgeon and myself were the first that arrived on the beach. The captain hailed us from the cabin window and let us know his disagreeable situation, telling us to force the Indians to put us on board. We having our muskets, they complied at once. Thus, by adding strength to the captain, we gained new assurance and, the others doing as we did, were put all on board as they came to the beach. The Indians offered no violence to the ship and when the crew were nearly all on board they began to leave the vessel, shipping off their booty.

Captain Portlock ordered us to take no notice of the transaction in way of hurting the Indians but to purchase back the articles they had taken away that were of use to us—but they had only taken what pieces of iron they found loose about the ship. After having hid the things they had stolen they began to trade as if nothing had happened, and we bought back what few bolts they had taken.

They had plundered the smith's tent in the same manner, although they looked upon him as a greater man than the captain. He was a smart young fellow and kept the Indians in great awe and wonder. They thought the coals were made into powder.* I have seen them steal small pieces and bruise them, then come back. When he saw this, he would spit upon the anvil while working the hot iron and give a blow upon it. They would run away in fear and astonishment when they heard the crack.

* Powder: gun powder.

7

*Trading Voyages—Conduct of the
Natives—Sandwich Islands—
Language—Nootka Sound—Ships
Sail for China.*

O NE OR OTHER of our boats, often both, were absent for some time upon trading voyages. In one of these trips our boat was nearly cut off, and would in all probability, had it not been for the presence of mind of an American, one of the crew, Joseph Laurence. I never was more alarmed for my safety in the whole voyage.

We were rowing through a lagoon to get a near cut to the ship. The tide was ebbing fast, the boat took the ground, and before we could do anything to get her off the whole bay was dry. The natives surrounded the boat in great numbers and looked very mischievous. We knew not what to do.

In this dilemma, Laurence, who knew their ways, took a small keg of molasses and went to the beach. At the same time he sat down by it and began to sing and lick, inviting them to follow his example. They licked and listened to him for a good while, and even joined him in singing—but the molasses wore done and they were weary of his songs.

We looked about in great anxiety and discovered a small height that commanded the boat. To this we ran but dared not to fire, even while they were plundering the boat. They could have killed us all with spears and stones, had we even shot one hundred of them and wasted all our ammunition.

We stood like bears at the stake, expecting them every moment to commence the attack, resolved to sell our lives as dear we could. At length the wished return of tide came and we got to the boat, and she floated soon after. Then we cared not one penny for them. We began to trade and bought back the articles they had stolen. Even our compass we were forced to buy back. We set sail for the *King George*, resolved to be more circumspect in future and happy we had escaped so well.

The party who had taken possession of the vessel on the Sabbath day, the next time they came back had their faces blacked and their heads powdered with the down of birds. They had done this as a disguise, which showed they had a consciousness of right and wrong. Thinking we knew them not, as we took no notice of them, they were as merry and funny as any of the rest.

While the boats were absent on a trading voyage the canoe was sent to haul the seine for salmon. There were fourteen men and boys in it. About half way between the vessel and the shore she filled with water. Those who could swim made for the beach. The boys, and those who could not, clung to the canoe. Captain Portlock saw from the deck the danger they were in and requested the boatswain, who was an excellent swimmer, to go to their assistance. He refused.

The sailmaker and myself leapt into the water. I had a line fixed round my waist, as I swam first, which he supported at a short distance behind, to ease its weight. When I came up to the canoe they were nearly spent. I fixed the line to the canoe and we made a signal to the ship when those on board drew her to the vessel, John Butler and I attending to assist and encourage them. There was a son of Sir John Dick's and a son of Captain Gore's among the boys. Captain Portlock never could bear the boatswain afterwards. Before this he was a great favourite.

While in Prince William's Sound the boat went on an excursion to Snug Corner Cove at the top of the Sound. She discovered the *Nootka*, Captain Mairs, in a most distressing situation from the scurvy. There were only the captain and two men free from disease. Two and twenty Lascars had died through the course of the winter. They had caused their own distress by their inordinate use of spirits on Christmas eve. They could not bury their own dead. They were only dragged a short distance from the ship and left upon the ice. They had muskets fixed upon the capstan and man-ropes that went down to the cabin, that when any of the natives attempted to come on board they might fire them off to scare them.

They had a large Newfoundland dog whose name was Towser, who alone kept the ship clear of the Indians. He lay day and night upon the ice before the cabin window, and would not allow the Indians to go into the ship. When the natives came to barter they would cry, '*Lally Towser*,' and make him a present of a skin before they began to trade with Captain Mairs, who lowered from the window his barter, and in the same way received their furs.

The *Beaver*, the *Nootka's* consort, had been cut off in the beginning of the winter and none of her people were ever heard of. We gave him every assistance in our power in spruce and molasses, and two of our crew to assist in working the vessel, Dickson and George Willis, who stopped at Canton until we arrived—then, wishing him well, took our leave of him. Captain Portlock could have made a fair prize of him, as he had no charter and was trading in our limits, but he was satisfied with his bond not to trade on our coast; but the bond was forfeit as soon as we sailed, and he was in China before us.

We now stood for Nootka Sound, but encountered a dreadful gale and were blown off the coast and suffered much in our sails and rigging which caused us to stand for the Sandwich Islands to refit—which gave us great joy.

The American coast is a hostile region compared with the Sandwich Islands. The American Indians are very jealous, and if any of our men were found with their women, using the least freedom, they would take his life if it was in their power; but their women are far from being objects of desire, they are so much disfigured by slitting their lips and placing large pieces of wood in them shaped like a saucer. I have seen them place berries upon it, and shake them into their mouth as a horse would corn out of a mouth-bag, or lick them in with their tongue. The men have a bone eight inches long, polished and stuck through the gristle of their nose. We called it their sprit-sailyard. We had suffered a good deal of hardship on this coast, and bade it adieu with joy.

Soon as we arrived at Owhyee our old acquaintance flocked on board to welcome us, each with a present. Then such a touching of noses and shaking of hands took place. '*Honi, honi*'—that is, touch nose, and 'How are you?'—were the only words to be heard. Our deck was one continued scene of joy. I was now picking up the language pretty fast and could buy and sell in it, and knew a great number of words that were very useful to me. There is a great likeness in many of their words to the Latin:

Sandwich Islands	English
terra	earth
nuna	moon
sola	sun
oma	man
leo	dog

Noue is their word for large, *maccou* for a fish-hook. When they saw our anchors they held up their hands and said, '*Noue maccou*.' During our wintering this second time, almost the same scenes were re-acted.

Having refitted and taken in provisions, we again set sail for Cook's River, Prince William's and Nootka Sound to obtain more fur skins. We were pretty successful. While on shore in Prince William's Sound, brewing spruce beer, I and the quartermaster made an excursion up the river and discovered a large space covered with snake-root, which is of great value in China.* My comrade, who had been in China,

* This was probably ginseng (*Panax spp.*) which has a forked root.

informed me of its value. It is the sweetest smelling plant I ever was near when it is growing. We set to work and dug up as much as we chose and dried it, letting no one know, for lessening the value of what we got. It was got safe on board the day before we sailed and we sold it well at Wampoa.*

We parted company from the *Queen Charlotte*. She had been absent for a long time. When a party of Indians came to the *King George*, having in their possession a pair of buckles that belonged to one of the people on board our consort, we became alarmed for her, thinking she had been cut off. We immediately set sail for Nootka Sound, leaving a large quantity of salmon half dried. After waiting in Nootka Sound, our place of rendezvous, for some time, and she not appearing, we immediately set sail for Owhyee, but got no word of our consort until we came to Atooi, when we perceived Abenoue in his single canoe, making her scud through the water, crying, '*Tattoo for Potipoti*,' as he jumped upon deck with a letter from Captain Dixon, which removed our fears and informed us he had discovered an island and got a very great number of skins and had sailed for China. We watered and laid in our provisions as quick as we could to follow her.

Abenoue, soon after he came on board, told the captain he had seen Billicany, and squinted so like Dickson we knew at once Mairs had been there in the

---

* Wampoa: a port town just outside Canton.

Nootka. Dickson afterwards told us Mairs would not have got anything from Abenoue had he and Willis not been with him.

Abenoue had a son called Poinoue—in English 'Large Pudding'. I thought him well named. He had the largest head of any boy I ever saw. His father wished Captain Portlock to take him to England but Poinoue did not wish to go. He leapt overboard just as we sailed and swam back to his father.

It was with a sensation of regret I bade a final adieu to the Sandwich Islands. Even now I would prefer them to any country I ever was in. The people so kind and obliging, the climate so fine and provisions so abundant—all render it a most endearing place.

Owhyee is the only place I was not ashore in. Captain Portlock never went himself and would not allow his crew to go. The murder of Cook made him timorous of trusting too much to the islanders. At Atooi and Onehow we went on shore, one watch one day, the other the next.

After taking on board as much provisions as we could stow we sailed for China. At the Ladrones, or Mariana Islands, a number of pilots came on board. The captain agreed with one. The bargain was made in the following manner. He showed the captain the number of dollars he wished by the number of cass, a small brass coin, the captain taking from the number what he thought too much, the pilot adding when he thought it too little. He was to pilot the *King George* to the island of Macau. From thence we sailed up the

Bocca Tigris to Wampoa, where we sold our cargo of skins.* We were engaged to take home a cargo of tea for the East India Company.

* Bocca Tigris: the estuary at the head of which Canton is situated.

8

China — Manners of the Chinese —
Food — Religion — Punishments —
Evasion of Duty — St Helena —
Author Arrives in England.

I WAS AS happy as any person ever was to see anything. I scarcely believed I was so fortunate as really to be in China. As we sailed up the river, I would cast my eyes from side to side. The thoughts and ideas I had pictured in my mind of it were not lessened in brilliancy, rather increased. The immense number of buildings that extended as far as the eye could reach, their fantastic shapes and gaudy colours, their trees and flowers so like their paintings, and the myriads of floating vessels, and above all the fanciful dresses and gaudy colours of their clothes—all serve to fix the mind of a stranger upon his first arrival. But upon a nearer acquaintance he is shocked at the quantity of individual misery that forces itself upon his notice, and gradually undoes the grand ideas he had formed of this strange people.

Soon as we cast anchor the vessel was surrounded with sampans. Every one had some request to make. Tartar girls requested our clothes to wash, barbers to shave the crews, others with fowls to sell; indeed, every necessary we could want. The first we made bargain with was a barber, Tommy Linn. He agreed to shave the crew for the six months we were to be there for half a dollar from each man, and he would shave every morning, if we chose, on board the ship, coming off in his sampan.

The Tartar girls washed our clothes for the broken meat or what rice we left at mess. They came every day in their sampans and took away the men's shirts, bringing them back the next, and never mixed the clothes. They all spoke less or more English and would jaw with the crew as fast as any women of their rank in England. They had a cage-like box fixed to the stern of their sampan in which was a pig who fed and fattened there at his ease.

Our ears were dinned with the cry of the beggars in their sampans, '*Kamscha me lillo rice*'. I have seen the mandarins plunder these objects of compassion when they had been successful in their appeals to the feelings of the seamen. I was surprised at the minute subdivision of their money. Their cass is a small piece of base coin with a square hole in it, three of which are a kandarin; sixty cass one mace; one mace equal to sevenpence English money. The cass is of no use out of the country, and when a seaman changes a dollar he receives no other coin from the wily Chinese.

I was on shore for a good while at Wampoa, making candle for our voyage home. I had a number of Chinese under me. My greatest difficulty was to prevent them from stealing the wax. They are greater and more dexterous thieves than the Indians. A bambooing for theft, I really believe, confers no disgrace upon them.

They will allow no stranger to enter the city of Canton. I was different times at the gate, but all my ingenuity could not enable me to cross the bar, although I was eight days in the suburbs. The Tartars are not even allowed to sleep on shore. They live in junks and other craft upon the river. If employed on shore they must be away by sunset, but may land again at sunrise in the morning.

The Chinese, I really believe, eat anything there is life in. Neptune was constantly on shore with me at the tent. Every night he caught less or more rats. He never eat them, but laid them down when dead at the tent door. In the morning the Chinese gave vegetables for them and were as well pleased as I was at the exchange.

After the candles were made I removed to Banks Hall to repair the cooper work, and screen sand and dry it, to pack the tea boxes for our voyage home. One day a boy was meddling rather freely with the articles belonging to me. Neptune bit him. I was extremely sorry for it, and after beating him dressed the boy's hurt which was not severe. I gave the boy a few cass, who went away quite pleased. In a short time after I saw him coming back, and his father leading him. I looked for squalls, but the father only asked a few hairs out from under Neptune's foreleg, close to the body. He would take them from no other part, and stuck them all over the wound.* He went away content. I had often heard, when a person had been tipsy the evening before, people tell him to take a hair of the dog that bit him, but never saw it in the literal sense before.

A short time before we sailed all the crew got two months' pay advance for private trade, and purchased

---

* Perhaps this was a folk preventative against rabies.

what articles they chose. The dollars are all stamped by the captain, as the Chinese are such cheats they will dexterously return you a bad dollar and assert, if not marked, it was the one you gave.

With all their roguery they are not ungrateful. One day two Chinese boys were playing in our boat. One of them fell overboard. The current was strong and the boy was carried down with rapidity. I leapt into the river and saved him with great difficulty, as the current bore us both along until my strength was almost spent. By an effort I got into the smooth water, and soon had the pleasure of delivering him to his father, who stood on the beach wringing his hands.

I wished to go on board, but the Chinese would have me to his house where I was most kindly received and got my dinner in great style. I like their manner of setting out the table at dinner. All that is to be eaten is placed upon the table at once, and all the liquors at the same time. You have all before you and you may make your choice. I dined in different houses and the same fashion was used in them all. The Chinese never thought he could show me kindness enough.

We buried our chief-mate, Mr Macleod, whose funeral I attended, upon French Island.

Almost every junk has a mandarin on board who keeps order and collects the revenue and tyrannises over the poor Chinese. They pay money for the liberty of doing anything to obtain a living. Tommy Linn paid seventy dollars for leave to practise as barber and surgeon upon the river.

They cure every disease by herbs. When any sailor or officer was so imprudent as visit Loblob Creek and received the reward of their folly, our surgeons could not cure them, yet the Chinese barber did so with ease.*

Every new moon all the men in China must have their heads shaved. If they do not the mandarin makes them suffer for it.

They have the longest nails to their fingers I ever saw. Many of their nails are half as long as the rest of the finger, they take so much care of them and keep them so white and clean. They, I really believe, would almost as soon have their throats cut as their nails. A Chinese will hold, by their means, more dollars in one hand than an Englishman will hold in both of his. Shaking hands will never be the fashion in China.

When the day is wet or thick, which rarely happens, the Chinese will say, 'Joss too much angry.' Then the paper sacrifices begin. The whole river is in a smoke. Every junk, down to the small sampan, must burn, under the direction of the mandarin, a certain quantity of paper to please 'Joss' their god. The rich must burn fine gilt paper, the poor coarser paper. The mandarin is the sole judge of the quantity and quality—from him there is no appeal. He himself burns no paper; a small piece of touchwood serves his turn. There he will stand in a conspicuous place, and look as steadfast upon it as a statue, until it is all burnt out.

* Loblob Creek: the local red-light district.

They are the most oppressed people I ever was amongst. They must want even a wife if they are not rich enough to pay the tax imposed by the mandarin. They are summary in their justice. Wherever the theft is committed, there the mandarin causes the culprit to be laid upon his back and beat upon the belly with a bamboo the number of times he thinks adequate to the offence. If the offence is great, they are sent to the Ladrone Islands, their place of banishment for thieves. There they live by piloting vessels and fishing but are not allowed to come up farther than Macau. They are cowardly and cruel. Six half-drunk sailors would clear a whole village; but when they catch one of them drunk and by himself, then they bamboo him in the cruellest manner.

Tommy Linn the barber was the agent we employed. He brought us any article we wanted from the city and, like his brethren in Europe, was a walking newspaper. His first word every morning was, 'Hey, yaw, what fashion?' and we used the same phrase to him. One morning he came, and the first thing he said was, 'Hey, yaw, what fashion? Soldier man's ship come to Lingcome bar.' We, after a few hours, heard that a man-of-war frigate had arrived at the mouth of the river. They are allowed to come no higher up. Tommy had seen the red coats of the marines.

They are much alarmed at the appearance of a man-of-war ship, and they often say, 'Englishman too much cruel, too much fight.' There were some

English seamen flogged for mutiny while we lay in the river. The Chinese wept like children for the men, saying, 'Hey, yaw, Englishman too much cruel, too much flog, too much flog.'

Having completed our cargo, we fell down the river. As we came near to the chop-house where the chop-marks are examined (the men having many articles on board in their private trade that had not paid duty, which the Chinese would have seized), we fell upon the old stratagem. When their boat put off two of us fell a fighting and we made the whole deck a scene of riot. These timorous Chinese custom-house-officers did not offer to come on board, but called out, 'Hey, yaw, what fashion? Too much baubry, too much baubry,' and put back to the chop-house.

By this manoeuvre we paid not one farthing of duty for our skins which we sold in China—the officers dared not come on board. We landed them as soon as possible and, when once in the factory, all was safe.

We set sail for St Helena where we made a present to the governor of a number of empty bottles. He in return gave us a present of potatoes, a valuable gift to us. While here, I and a number of the crew were nearly poisoned by eating albicores and bonettos.* We split and hung them in the rigging to dry. The moon's rays have the effect of making them

---

* Albicores and bonettos: fish similar to tuna and mackerel.

poisonous. My face turned red and swelled, but the others were far worse. Their heads were swelled twice their ordinary size—but we all recovered.

In a few days we set sail for England where I arrived without any remarkable occurrence after an absence of three years, having in that time circum-navigated the globe. We came into the river in the month of September 1788.

9

Author Engaged as Steward of a Convict Ship—Anecdotes of Female Convicts—Sails for New South Wales—Attaches Himself to Sarah Whitlam—Singular Punishment—Crossing the Line—Miscellaneous Occurrences—Port Jackson—St Helena.

I NOW RETURNED to Scotland with a sensation of joy only to be felt by those who have been absent for some time. Every remembrance was rendered more dear, every scene was increased in beauty. A piece of oaten cake tasted far sweeter in my mouth than the luxuries of eastern climes.

I was for a time reconciled to remain. The love of country overcame my wandering habits. I had some thought of settling for life, as I had saved a good deal of my pay. In the middle of these musings, and before I had made up my mind, a letter I received from Captain Portlock upset all my future plans and rekindled my wandering propensities with as great vigour as ever.

The letter requested me to come to London without delay, as there were two ships lying in the river bound for New South Wales: the *Guardian* and *Lady Julian*, in either of which I might have a berth.* The *Guardian* was loaded with stores and necessaries for the settlement. There was a vine-dresser and a person to superintend the cultivation of hemp on board. She sailed long before us. The *Lady Julian* was to take out female convicts.

I would have chosen the *Guardian*, only she was a man-of-war, and as I meant to settle in Scotland upon our return I could not have left her when I chose. My only object was to see the country, not to remain at sea. I therefore chose the *Lady Julian*, as she was a

---

* This was the *Lady Juliana* which sailed with the second fleet.

transport, although I did not by any means like her cargo—yet to see the country I was resolved to submit to a great deal.

I was appointed steward of the *Lady Julian*, commanded by Captain Aitkin, who was an excellent humane man and did all in his power to make the convicts as comfortable as their circumstances would allow. The government agent, an old lieutenant, had been discharged a little before I arrived for cruelty to the convicts. He had even begun to flog them in the river. Government, the moment they learned the fact, appointed another in his place.

We lay six months in the river before we sailed, during which time all the jails in England were emptied to complete the cargo of the *Lady Julian*. When we sailed there were on board 245 female convicts.* There were not a great many very bad characters. The greater number were for petty crimes, and a great proportion for only being disorderly, that is, street-walkers, the colony at the time being in great want of women.

One, a Scottish girl, broke her heart and died in the river. She was buried at Dartford. Four were pardoned on account of his Majesty's recovery. The poor young Scottish girl I have never yet got out of my mind. She was young and beautiful, even in the convict dress, but pale as death, and her eyes red with weeping.

* The *Lady Juliana* actually carried 226 convicts.

She never spoke to any of the other women or came on deck. She was constantly seen sitting in the same corner from morning to night. Even the time of meals roused her not. My heart bled for her—she was a countrywoman in misfortune. I offered her consolation but her hopes and heart had sunk. When I spoke she heeded me not, or only answered with sighs and tears. If I spoke of Scotland she would wring her hands and sob until I thought her heart would burst. I endeavoured to get her sad story from her lips but she was silent as the grave to which she hastened. I lent her my Bible to comfort her but she read it not. She laid it on her lap after kissing it, and only bedewed it with her tears. At length she sunk into the grave of no disease but a broken heart. After her death we had only two Scottish women on board, one of them a Shetlander.

I went every day to the town to buy fresh provisions and other necessaries for them. As their friends were allowed to come on board to see them, they brought money; and numbers had it of their own, particularly a Mrs Barnsley, a noted sharper and shoplifter.* She herself told me her family for one

---

* Elizabeth Barnsley was fashionably dressed and 'had every appearance of gentility' when she visited an expensive draper's shop in Bond Street in February 1788, in the company of Ann Wheeler. They bought some muslin and Irish cloth, but a shop assistant noticed that Wheeler had slipped a whole bolt of muslin under her cloak and muff. Both women were convicted of theft, and Elizabeth spent over a year in

hundred years back had been swindlers and highway-
men. She had a brother, a highwayman, who often
came to see her as well dressed and genteel in his
appearance as any gentleman. She petitioned the
government agent and captain to be allowed to wear
her own clothes in the river, and not the convict dress.
This could on no account be allowed, but they told
her she might wear what she chose when once they
were at sea.

The agent, Lieutenant Edgar, had been with
Captain Cook, was a kind humane man and very good
to them. He had it in his power to throw all their
clothes overboard when he gave them the convict
dress, but he gave them to me to stow in the after
hold, saying, 'They would be of use to the poor creatures when they arrived at Port Jackson.'

Those from the country came all on board in irons,
and I was paid half a crown a head by the country jailors,
in many cases, for striking them off upon my anvil, as they
were not locked but riveted. There was a Mrs Davis, a
noted swindler, who had obtained great quantities of
goods under false names and other equally base means.*

* Two women with the surname of Davis were on board the
Lady Juliana. The younger, Ann, was sentenced to seven

Newgate prison where she paid half a crown a week to stay
in a relatively comfortable part of the prison. She joined her
husband in Sydney where she bore him two sons. The family
presumably returned to England after 1795. (See Michael
Flynn, *The Second Fleet: Britain's Grim Convict Armada of
1790*, Library of Australian History, Sydney, 1993, 150.)

We had one Mary Williams, transported for receiving stolen goods.* She and other eight had been a long time in Newgate where Lord George Gordon had supported them. I went once a week to him and got their allowance from his own hand all the time we lay in the river.

One day I had the painful task to inform the father and mother of one of the convicts that their daughter, Sarah Dorset, was on board. They were decent-looking people, and had come to London to inquire after her. When I met them they were at Newgate. The jailor referred them to me. With tears in her eyes the mother implored me to tell her if such a one was on board. I told them there was one of that name. The father's heart seemed too full to allow him to speak but the mother with streaming eyes blessed God that they had found their poor lost child, undone as she was.

---

* Two convicts named Mary Williams sailed with Nicol. The one apparently referred to by Nicol had a tragic story to tell. Desperate to pay the rent of half a crown per week due on her room, she pawned a pair of sheets, two blankets and a pillow belonging to the room. She was sentenced to seven years' transportation but spent eighteen months in Newgate prison waiting for the sentence to be carried out. She was twenty-four when she embarked on the *Lady Juliana*. (See *The Second Fleet*, 613.)

---

years' transportation for trying to sell stolen clothing. The older, Deborah, had been sentenced to death (later commuted to transportation) for stealing jewellery from Mr Timothy Topping of Chislehurst. It is probably Deborah that Nicol is talking of here. (See *The Second Fleet*, 235-36.)

I called a coach, drove to the river and had them put on board. The father, with a trembling step, mounted the ship's side, but we were forced to lift the mother on board. I took them down to my berth and went for Sarah Dorset. When I brought her the father said in a choking voice, 'My lost child!' and turned his back, covering his face with his hands. The mother, sobbing, threw her hands around her. Poor Sarah fainted and fell at their feet. I knew not what to do. At length she recovered and in the most heart-rending accents implored their pardon.

She was young and pretty and had not been two years from her father's house at this present time, so short had been her course of folly and sin. She had not been protected by the villain that ruined her above six weeks, then she was forced by want upon the streets and taken up as a disorderly girl, then sent on board to be transported. This was her short but eventful history. One of our men, William Power, went out to the colony when her time was expired, brought her home and married her.*

I witnessed many moving scenes, and many of the most hardened indifference. Numbers of them would

---

* Sarah Dorset was convicted of stealing a greatcoat from a London pub. She was sentenced to seven years' transportation. Sarah in fact bore a son to Edward Powell, a seaman on the *Lady Juliana*. Powell did return to Sydney in 1793 but he then married Elizabeth Fish, a free woman, who returned with him to England. Sarah became housekeeper to John Woodward, butcher. The couple had three children. Sarah died in New South Wales in 1838. (See *The Second Fleet*, 248.)

not take their liberty as a boon. They were thankful for their present situation, so low had vice reduced them. Many of these from the country jails had been allowed to leave it to assist in getting in the harvest, and voluntarily returned.

When I inquired their reason, they answered, 'How much more preferable is our present situation to what it has been since we commenced our vicious habits? We have good victuals and a warm bed. We are not ill treated or at the mercy of every drunken ruffian as we were before. When we rose in the morning we knew not where we would lay our heads in the evening, or if we would break our fast in the course of the day. Banishment is a blessing for us. Have we not been banished for a long time, and yet in our native land, the most dreadful of all situations? We dared not go to our relations whom we had disgraced. Other people would shut their doors in our faces. We were as if a plague were upon us, hated and shunned.'

Others did all in their power to make their escape. These were such as had left their associates in rapine on shore and were hardened to every feeling but the abandoned enjoyments of their companions. Four of these made their escape on the evening before we left England through the assistance of their confederates on shore. They gave the man on watch gin to drink as he sat on the quarterdeck, the others singing and making fun. These four slipped over her bows into a boat provided for their escape. I never heard if they were retaken. We sailed without them.

Mrs Nelly Kerwin, a female of daring habits, banished for life for forging seamen's powers of attorney and personating their relations, when on our passage down the river, wrote to London for cash to some of her friends.* She got a letter informing her it was waiting for her at Dartmouth. We were in Colson Bay when she got this letter. With great address she persuaded the agent that there was an express for him and money belonging to her lying at Dartmouth. A man was sent who brought on board Nell's money, but no express for the agent. When she got it she laughed in his face and told him he was in her debt for a lesson. He was very angry, as the captain often told him Kerwin was too many for him.

We had on board a girl pretty well behaved, who was called by her acquaintance a daughter of Pitt's.**

---

* Eleanor Kirvein kept a 'house of entertainment for sailors' at Gosport. An important part of her business was 'bomb-boating'—providing credit and accommodation for sailors and finding them berths on outward-bound ships. She was convicted of forging the will of a seaman and was sentenced to death. After a 'panel of matrons' found her to be pregnant her sentence was commuted to transportation for seven years. She married Henry Palmer, a convict, in July 1790. A few months later he was killed by a falling tree. She sailed for India, a free woman, in 1793. Michael Flynn notes that she was probably one of the few convict mothers who lived to see the children they left behind. (See *The Second Fleet*, 386.)

** William Pitt (1759-1806) was the current prime minister of Great Britain.

She herself never contradicted it. She bore a most striking likeness to him in every feature and could scarce be known from him as to looks. We left her at Port Jackson.

Some of our convicts I have heard even to boast of the crimes and murders committed by them and their accomplices, but the far greater number were harmless unfortunate creatures, the victims of the basest seduction. With their histories, as told by themselves, I shall not trouble the reader.

When we were fairly out to sea, every man on board took a wife from among the convicts, they nothing loath. The girl with whom I lived, for I was as bad in this point as the others, was named Sarah Whitlam. She was a native of Lincoln, a girl of a modest reserved turn, as kind and true a creature as ever lived. I courted her for a week and upwards, and would have married her on the spot had there been a clergyman on board.

She had been banished for a mantle she had borrowed from an acquaintance. Her friend prosecuted her for stealing it, and she was transported for seven years.*

---

* Sarah Whitlam, who was born in 1767, was in fact convicted of the theft of a large amount of cloth and clothing, including six yards of black chintz cotton, a raven grey Coventry tammy gown, a pink quilted petticoat, a pair of stays, a fine white lawn apron, a chocolate ground silk handkerchief, a woman's black silk hat and a pair of leather shoes. Flynn speculates that her loot would have filled a cart and may have been stolen from a shop. (See *The Second Fleet*, 610.)

I had fixed my fancy upon her from the moment I knocked the rivet out of her irons upon my anvil, and as firmly resolved to bring her back to England when her time was out, my lawful wife, as ever I did intend anything in my life. She bore me a son in our voyage out.

What is become of her, whether she is dead or alive, I know not. That I do not is no fault of mine, as my narrative will show.

But to proceed. We soon found that we had a troublesome cargo, yet not dangerous or very mischievous—as I may say, more noise than danger. When any of them, such as Nance Ferrel who was ever making disturbance, became very troublesome we confined them down in the hold and put on the hatch.* This, we were soon convinced, had no effect as they became in turns outrageous, on purpose to be confined. Our agent and the captain wondered at the change in their behaviour.

I, as steward, found it out by accident. As I was overhauling the stores in the hold I came upon a hogshead of bottled porter with a hole in the side of it and, in place of full, there were nothing but empty bottles in it. Another was begun and more than a box of candles had been carried off. I immediately told the captain, who now found out the

---

* Elizabeth Farrell was convicted of stealing clothing and linen from a house in East Smithfield. She eventually went to Van Diemen's Land where she lived comfortably with her husband John Hall, a first-fleet convict. She died in Hobart in 1827. (See *The Second Fleet*, 268.)

cause of the late insubordination and desire of confinement.

We were forced to change the manner of punishing them. I was desired by the agent Lieutenant Edgar, who was an old lieutenant of Cook's, to take a flour barrel and cut a hole in the top for their head and one on each side for their arms. This we called a wooden jacket. Next morning, Nance Ferrel, as usual, came to the door of the cabin and began to abuse the agent and captain. They desired her to go away between decks and be quiet. She became worse in her abuse, wishing to be confined and sent to the hold, but to her mortification the jacket was produced, and two men brought her upon deck and put it on.

She laughed and capered about for a while, and made light of it. One of her comrades lighted a pipe and gave it her. She walked about strutting and smoking the tobacco, and making the others laugh at the droll figure she made. She walked a minuet, her head moving from side to side like a turtle.

The agent was resolved she should be heartily tired, and feel in all its force the disagreeableness of her present situation. She could only walk or stand— to sit or lie down was out of her power. She began to get weary and begged to be released. The agent would not until she asked his pardon, and promised amendment in future. This she did in humble terms before evening, but in a few days was as bad as ever. There was no taming her by gentle means. We were forced to tie her up like a man, and give her one dozen with the cat-o'-nine-tails, and assure her of a clawing every offence. This alone reduced her to any kind of order.

How great was the contrast between her and Mary Rose. Mary was a timid modest girl who never joined in the ribaldry of the rest, neither did she take up with any man upon the voyage. She was a wealthy farmer's daughter who had been seduced under promise of marriage by an officer, and had eloped with him from her father's house. They were living together in Lincoln when the officer was forced to go abroad and leave her. He, before he went, boarded her with their landlady, an infamous character, who, to obtain the board she had received in advance without maintaining the unfortunate girl, swore she had robbed her of several articles.

Poor Mary was condemned by her perjury and sentenced to be transported. She had disgraced her friends and dared not apply to them in her distress. She had set the opinions of the world at defiance by her elopement, and there was no one in it who appeared to befriend her, while in all its bitterness she drank the cup of her own mixing. After the departure of the *Lady Julian* her relations had discovered the fate of their lost and ruined Mary. By their exertions the whole scene of the landlady's villainy was exposed, and she stood in the pillory at Lincoln for her perjury.

Upon our arrival we found a pardon lying at Port Jackson, and a chest of excellent clothes sent by the magistrates for her use in the voyage home. She lodged all the time I was there in the governor's house and every day I took her allowance to her. She was to sail in the first ship for London direct, the *Lady Julian* being bound for China. During the tedious voyage out I took her under my protection. Sarah and she were acquaint before they saw each other in misfortune. Mary washed the clothes and did any little thing for Sarah when she was confined, which she was long before we reached Port Jackson.*

The first place we stopped at was Santa Cruz in the island of Tenerife for water. As we used a great

---

* Mary Rose had the most extraordinary career of any of the convict women mentioned by Nicol. At sixteen she was sentenced to seven years' transportation for stealing clothes. Fortune had smiled upon her, however, in giving her such a romantic and patriotic name. It seems that it never failed to elicit sympathy in her hour of need. Michael Flynn observes that Nicol's view of her 'mixes fact with romantic fiction' but that 'he was not the only one to fall under her spell'.

Following her imprisonment in Lincoln an anonymous poet penned a romantic ballad to publicise her plight. This it seems was associated with a plea for clemency from no less a person than Sir Joseph Banks! Nicol's assertion that a pardon and clothing were waiting for her in Port Jackson is clearly impossible, as no vessel arrived in the settlement from England between the first and second fleets.

Nicol may have been misled by the fact that Governor Phillip was aware of Banks' plea, and arranged for Rose to marry 'one of the best men in this place'. Less than a year later Phillip lamented to Banks that 'my desire of making her better has only been the means of ruining the poor devil who married her'. Rose lived on in Sydney until at least 1825. (See *The Second Fleet*, 508.)

quantity the agent, at the captain's request, had laid
in tea and sugar in place of beef or pork allowed by
government. We boiled a large kettle of water that
served the whole convicts and crew every night and
morning. We allowed them water for washing their
clothes, any quantity they chose, while in port. Many
times they would use four and five boatloads in one
day.

We did not restrain the people on shore from
coming on board through the day. The captains and
seamen who were in port at the time paid us many
visits. Mrs Barnsley bought a cask of wine and got
it on board with the agent's leave. She was very kind
to her fellow convicts who were poor. They were all
anxious to serve her. She was as a queen among
them.

We had a number of Jewesses on board. One,
Sarah Sabolah, had a crucifix, and the others soon got
them and passed themselves for Roman Catholics, by
which means they got many presents from the people
on shore and laid up a large stock for sea.*

We next stood for Sao Tiago, accompanied by two
slave ships from Santa Cruz to Sao Tiago, who sailed
thus far out of their course for the sake of the ladies.
They came on board every day when the weather
would permit. At length they stood for the coast to
pick up their cargo of human misery. We watered

* Sarah Sabolah cannot be traced. The name may have been
an assumed one.

again and made all clear for a new start. Our Jewesses played off the same farce with their crucifixes, and with equal success.

We then stood for Rio de Janeiro where we lay eight weeks taking in coffee and sugar, our old stock being now reduced very low. I was employed on shore repairing flour casks to receive it. The Jewesses made here a good harvest, and the ladies had a constant run of visitors. I had received fifty suits of child-bed linen for their use—they were a present from the ladies of England. I here served out twenty suits. Mrs Barnsley acted as midwife and was to practise at Port Jackson, but there was no clergyman on board. When in port the ladies fitted up a kind of tent for themselves.

In crossing the line we had the best sport I ever witnessed upon the same occasion. We had caught a porpoise the day before the ceremony which we skinned to make a dress for Neptune with the tail stuffed. When he came on deck he looked the best representation of a merman I ever saw, painted, with a large swab upon his head for a wig. Not a man in the ship could have known him. One of the convicts fainted, she was so much alarmed at his appearance, and had a miscarriage after. Neptune made the boys confess their amours to him, and I was really astonished at the number. I will not describe the ceremony to fatigue the reader, as it has been often described by others.*

---

* The ceremony of crossing the Equator was an occasion of
  much merriment. Often the oldest and ugliest sailor was

From Rio de Janeiro we sailed for the Cape of Good Hope, where we took on board seventy-three ewes and a ram for the settlement. We were detained a long time here as we found that the *Guardian* had struck upon an island of ice, and was so severely injured that she was deserted by most of her crew, who were never heard of afterwards. The captain and those who remained with him in the ship were only saved by being towed into the Cape by an American vessel. What detained us was the packing of flour and other necessaries for the colony, as we knew it must be in great want, the *Guardian* being loaded with supplies for it.

At length we sailed for Port Jackson. We made one of the convicts shepherdess, who was so fortunate in her charge of the flock as not to lose one. While we lay at the Cape we had a narrow escape from destruction by fire. The carpenter allowed the pitch-pot to boil over upon the deck, and the flames rose in an alarming manner. The shrieks of the women were dreadful, and the confusion they made running about drove everyone stupid. I ran to my berth, seized a pair of blankets to keep it down until the others drowned it with water. Captain Aitkin made me a handsome present for my exertions.

The captain had a quantity of linen on board, and during the voyage had kept above twenty of the

---

dressed up as King Neptune's wife, and another as Neptune himself. Many liberties were taken with the crew and the officers.

convicts making shirts to sell at Port Jackson. He got them made cheap and sold them to great advantage upon our arrival as the people of the colony were in want of every necessity.

At length, almost to our sorrow, we made the land upon the 3rd of June 1790, just one year all but one day from our leaving the river. We landed all our convicts safe. My charge as steward did not expire for six weeks after our arrival, as the captain, by agreement, was bound to victual them during that time.

It is a fine country and everything thrives well in it. A sergeant of marines supplied the *Lady Julian* with potatoes and garden stuffs for half a crown a day. There were thirty-six people on board and we had as much as we could use. There were only two natives in the town at the time, a boy and a girl.* These had been brought in by a party of the settlers, having been left by their parents. I saw but little of the colony, as my time was fully occupied in my duties as steward, and any moments I could spare I gave them to Sarah.

The days flew on eagles' wings, for we dreaded the hour of separation which at length arrived. It was not without the aid of the military we were brought on board. I offered to lose my wages but we were short of hands, one man having been left sick at Rio de Janeiro, and we had lost our carpenter

---

* They were Abaroo and Nanbaree, survivors of the smallpox epidemic, who were then living with Surgeon White (Nanbaree) and the Reverend and Mrs Johnson (Abaroo).

who fell overboard. The captain could not spare a man and requested the aid of the governor. I thus was forced to leave Sarah, but we exchanged faith. She promised to remain true, and I promised to return when her time expired and bring her back to England.*

I wished to have stolen her away, but this was impossible, the convicts were so strictly guarded by the marines. There were no soldiers in the colony at this time. With a heavy heart I bade adieu to Port Jackson, resolved to return as soon as I reached England. We would have remained some time longer, but Captain Aitkin was very unwell and the mate was anxious to complete the voyage.

They have an herb in the colony they call sweet tea.** It is infused and drank like the China tea. I liked it much. It requires no sugar and is both a bitter and a sweet. There was an old female convict, her hair quite grey with age, her face shrivelled, who was suckling a child she had borne in the colony. Everyone went to see her, and I among the rest. It was a strange sight. Her hair was quite white. Her fecundity was ascribed to the sweet tea.

---

* John Nicol and Sarah Whitlam parted for the last time on 25 July 1790. On 26 July Sarah married John Coen Walsh, a first-fleet convict. She signed the marriage register with a cross. In June 1796 the couple sailed for England via India with their two sons. Walsh was back in Australia by 1801 but there are no further records of Sarah Whitlam.

** *Smilax glyciphylla.*

I brought away with me two bags of it as presents to my friends, but two of our men became very ill of the scurvy and I allowed them the use of it, which soon cured them but reduced my store. When we came to China I showed it to my Chinese friends, and they bought it with avidity and importuned me for it and a quantity of the seed I had likewise preserved. I let them have the seed, and only brought a small quantity of the herb to England.

Upon our arrival at Wampoa I renewed my acquaintance with my Chinese friends, and was as happy as I could be with the thoughts of Sarah's situation upon my mind—but this was the dullest voyage I ever made. I changed my berth in the ship, but all would not do. Everything brought her endearing manners to my recollection. To leave her a convict was a great aggravation to my grief. Had I left her by choice for a voyage I could have thought of her with pleasing regret and anxious hope of seeing her soon. But to leave her exposed to temptation in the very worst company the world could produce was too much to think of with composure. I left with her my Bible, the companion of all my voyages, with our names written in it. She used to read it often, when I never thought of it.

So much did these thoughts prey upon my mind I almost resolved to lose my wages by leaving the *Lady Julian* at Rio or the Cape. But to be so far from home, without one penny in my pocket to pay her passage to England, would have been madness, as I could not bear the idea of bidding for ever farewell to Scotland, the place where my wanderings were always intended to cease.

I made up my mind to come to England in the *Lady Julian*, and get a berth out the first opportunity, and by that time her term of transportation would be expired. We touched at St Helena on our way to England. When we arrived I was paid off and immediately made every inquiry for a ship for New Holland, but there was none, nor any likely to be soon.

10

Author Engaged on Board a South Sea Whaler—Miscellaneous Occurrences—Grief at the Conduct of Sarah—Seal-Fishing—Sea Lions—Unexpectedly Meets a Countryman at Paita—Transactions There.

THERE WAS A vessel called the *Amelia*, Captain Shiels, fitting out as a south-sea whaler. She belonged to Squire Enderborough, Paul's Wharf, London. I got myself engaged as cooper of her. The whole crew were on shares. I, as cooper, had a larger share than a seaman, but this was not my present aim, neither did I think of gain.

I had all my money secured about my person, sewed into my clothes, ready for a start, and with it to pay the passage of Sarah and my son to England. My intention was, when we arrived at Rio de Janeiro on our return home, to fall sick and endeavour to obtain my share from the captain and allow the vessel to sail without me, or to claim it when I reached England. From Rio I could easily get a ship to the Cape. From the Cape to New South Wales I had the only chance of a vessel. I would have remained until the *Amelia* reached the Cape, but she might not even anchor there. These were my views in entering on board the *Amelia*.

In two months after my leaving the *Lady Julian* I was again at sea in hopes of reaching Port Jackson by some means or other. In our first offset we were stranded upon the Red Sand near the Nore. While we lay in distress, the Deal men came out and wished to make a wreck of us by cutting away our masts.* I, with

---

* Deal was one of the 'cinque ports' near Dover. The men of Deal were pilots, lifeboat men and smugglers known for 'hovelling', or taking disabled ships.

alacrity, aided the captain and stood guard with a brace of pistols, and threatened to blow out the brains of the first man of them that offered to set his foot upon our deck.

The weather fortunately was moderate. We, having no longboat, carried out our anchor between two boats into deep water, and as the tide flowed we got her off. To my great disappointment we were forced to put back into dock to have her examined by removing the copper sheathing. All the crew left her except myself, as the engagement was broken by our return to dock, and the men would not continue in her as they thought no good would come of the voyage. Her stranding was an omen of her bad luck.

There was no ship in the river for New South Wales, and the Indiamen would not sail until about the month of March. The *Amelia* would still be the first vessel. I had no inducement, therefore, to leave her.

We were soon again ready for sea, and set sail with an entire new crew. The first land we made was the island of Buena Vista which belongs to the Portuguese, where we took in livestock, and salt to salt down our seal skins, then stood for Sao Tiago and took in more livestock; from thence to the Falkland Islands for geese and swine. We next made Staten Island, and passed the Straits of Magellan and Straits le Mair, but did not go through either of them. We doubled the Cape then stood down to our fishing ground which was between latitude 18° and the Line.

We had nothing to do but commence, as we had been busy all the voyage preparing and fitting our tackle. Our boilers were fitted up before we left England as in the south seas the spermaceti is all boiled upon the deck. The boiler is built up with fire brick, and a space left between the lower tier and the deck about nine inches high, quite watertight. When once the fire is kindled, which is never after allowed to go out until the ship is fully fished, the space between the bricks and the deck is kept full of water. There are two plug-holes (one on each side) so that when the water heats and would melt the pitch, upon whatever tack the ship may be, the plug is drawn from the under side and the space immediately filled with cold water from the higher side. Great attention is required to watch the boilers. We do not require to carry out fuel to boil our oil, as the refuse of the oil is used ever after the first fire is kindled.

The ashes of the fire is better than any soap. Let our clothes be ever so black and greasy, as they must be from our employment, one shovel full of ashes in a tub of water will make them as clean as when we bought them.

During the fishing we lived wholly upon turtle and were heartily tired of them. We were very fortunate in our fishing. We caught one whale from which we obtained 125 pounds weight of ambergrease, the largest quantity ever brought to England by one ship.

Upon the fishing ground we found the *Venus*, Captain Coffin. She had taken out convicts to Port

Jackson and there was a convict on board at the time. He had concealed himself in her until she was at sea, and by this means made his escape from the colony. He used to hide himself from me but, the other men assuring him I would not inform, he had the courage to speak to me at length, and inquired if ever I had been at Port Jackson.

I told him I had in the *Lady Julian*. He answered he had seen me there. My heart beat high with anxiety. I feared, yet wished, to hear of Sarah Whitlam.

At length I inquired. How shall I express my grief when informed she had left the colony for Bombay. Thus were my worst fears realised. Unconstant woman! Why doubt my faith? Yet dear, and never to be forgotten, I resolved to follow her to India. I could not speak to him so broke off the conversation for the present and left him in greater despondency than I left Port Jackson. My grief was not then mixed with doubts of her constancy. She had only three years to serve when I left her, and these were not yet expired. How she got away he could not inform me.

Every time we met I renewed my inquiries. He was so uniform in his replies, and assured me of its truth so solemnly, I was forced to believe the unpleasant truth. I inquired for my son John, but he could give me no information to be relied on. He believed she had taken him with her but, as the children are taken from the convicts and maintained at school by the government, he knew not her son from the others, and did not see her go away.

I now had no inducement to go to Port Jackson and for a few days scarce cared what became of me. My love for her revived stronger at this time than any other since I left her. I even gave her praise for leaving it. She did so to be out of bad company, my mind would whisper, and I resolved to get to Bombay as soon as possible, and endeavour to find her out.

As my usual buoyancy of spirits returned, I pursued my labours with all the ardour of a seaman. After taking a sufficient quantity of spermaceti we stood as far down as latitude 3° to the Island of Lopes where we killed thirty thousand seals.* We had a busy time chasing and killing them. When we had a sufficient number we began to kill sea-lions to get their skins for the ship's use. One of their skins was a sufficient load for two men. We used to stand in a gap of the rocks in the morning and knock them down with our clubs as they approached the sea, then stab them with our long knives.

George Parker our mate made a blow at one and missed him. He made a snap at George and sent his tusk right through his arm, a little above the wrist, and walked away at his leisure with him into the sea, Parker roaring like a bull from the pain and terror. Robert Wyld, perceiving his danger, rushed into the water to rescue him, and was up to the armpits before

---

* Island of Lopes: Lobos Island in northern Peru.

he succeeded in dispatching the unwieldy monster. He then dragged them both on shore where, with difficulty, the tusk was drawn from between the bones, it was so firmly jammed.

We soon after sailed three degrees to the north of the Line to the River Tambo where we anchored, and the captain ascended the river nine miles in his boat, to which I belonged, to the town of Tambo. We had an American Indian for a pilot. He appeared to worship the alligators as he kept constantly bowing and muttering to them, and a busy time he had of it as they were very numerous.

The governor of the town and people were very kind and civil to us. We remained all night at the governor's house, feasting like kings. Captain Shiels made him a present of some porter and a cheese and a few other things, for which he would have given us as many bullocks as we chose. We only took one which was as much as we could use fresh, there being only sixteen hands in the ship. We watered in the river then crossed the Line to the city of Paita, where we anchored in a beautiful bay, quite land-locked and as smooth as a mill-pond.

We scarcely had made all tight when a boat came alongside, and inquired if there was a Scotchman on board. The captain allowed me to go as I was the only one in the ship. I was conducted to a baker's shop in the town and into an elegant room, where a sickly-looking person, but elegantly dressed, rose and met me, shaked hands, and said, 'How's a' wi' you?'

My ears tingled and my heart leapt for joy to hear the accents of my native tongue so unexpectedly. I looked hard at him but had never seen him before. I thanked him and we sat down together and began a long conversation. We talked of Old Scotland and the talk was all on my side for a long while, he had so many questions to put, and he seemed to devour every word I spoke while joy beamed in his sickly features.

At length I got his own history. He was a native of Inverness and had been bred to the sea and, coming to the West Indies, had engaged in the contraband trade carried on along the Spanish main; had been taken prisoner and carried to Montevideo; from thence to Lima where he had been long in prison and suffered many hardships but, being a Roman Catholic, he was not sent to the mines. He had found means to obtain his liberty and afterwards win the love of a rich Spanish lady who procured him his pardon and afterwards married him. He was now very rich and had a ship of his own, besides immense property, but having fallen sick at Paita he had ordered his vessel to proceed on her voyage and send his servants to carry him overland to Lima. He was expecting them every day.

He treated me nobly and made me a handsome present when he went away, which he did while we lay at Paita. I was astonished at the number of servants and horses that came for him. His saddle would have bought fifty horses. The stirrups were solid gold, and every part was loaded with it. The maker seemed to have studied more to lay on gold than taste in the ornaments. He made the most enticing offers to induce me to go with him, but Sarah was dearer to me than all the riches in the world.

The governor and people of Paita were so kind to us we passed our time very agreeably. All their houses were open to us. They forced presents of fruit upon us, and gave us as much accadent as we chose to drink.*

The governor treated us with a Spanish play. These entertainments are through the day. During the performance we were served with wine, sweet-meats and fruits, but not understanding the language we paid more attention to the refreshments than the play. The governor was one of the kindest gentlemen I ever saw. He told us he loved the English for their humanity; he had been in the town when Lord Anson plundered it.** Ever since they do not keep their saints and plate in the church, but in the town-house which is no stronger than the church. You may see them carrying it back and forward every day.

The governor was very anxious to learn English. I could buy and sell in Spanish. Upon this account he took great notice of me. I had a Spanish and English dictionary on board. I gave it him, and he made me a

---

* Accadent: spiritous liquor.
** Admiral Anson sailed upon a voyage around the world in the years 1740–44, during which he plundered Paita but showed the inhabitants great mercy.

handsome present he was so much pleased with it—
and he made rapid progress in his study.

He was the first that told me of the King of
France's death. He said, drawing his hand across his
neck, 'The people have cut the neck of de Roi de
Française.' I understood what he meant, but did not
believe the information.

I wore in general, when ashore, a black jacket with
black horn buttons. A priest I used often to meet at
the governor's took a fancy to the buttons and offered
me any price for them. I soon cut off my buttons, and
gave them to him. I had breeches and vest with the
same buttons; off went they, every one. A Jew would
have counted it a good bargain.

Amidst all their kindness they are very superstitious. I must have lain in the streets all night one
evening I missed the boat, had not a Portuguese who
was with me told them I was an Irishman. 'O bon
Irelandois! O bon Christian!' they cried and made me
welcome, gave me the best in the house, happy to
entertain so good a Christian as an Irishman.

While everything was going on to our wish, and
our ambergrease selling well, we were forced to leave
Paita in great haste. One of our men, getting himself tipsy, told the people openly we were selling
ambergrease and had still a great quantity to sell.
The governor immediately sent for the captain and
informed him of his danger. He himself was not against
the sale but should word reach Lima they would
order a frigate to Paita and make a prize of us. We

were too much afraid of this to tarry longer than get in what supplies we stood in need of, for which the governor would accept no payment.

I went with other two to take leave of the governor. As we proceeded along we saw two ladies swinging in a net, and a female servant keeping it in motion. We stood looking at them a few minutes before they perceived us. As soon as they did they desired the servant to cease, came down and bade us come into the house where they treated us with fruit and wine, and would scarce allow us to go away so soon as we wanted. The ladies here have a pale and sickly look. All their movements are languid. Even the men are far from being active. Everyone moves as if he wished someone to carry him.

11

Rio de Janeiro—Portuguese Seamen—Lisbon—Author Arrives in London—Visits Sarah's Parents— Enters a Vessel Bound for China— Anecdote.

WHEN WE SAILED we had two booms over our stern, and a net made fast to them filled with pumpkins, melons and other vegetables, the gift of these kind Spaniards. We stood direct for Rio de Janeiro, where Captain Shiels intended to remain for some time as he had completed his cargo so soon. He would have lost the bounty had he arrived before the time specified in the act of parliament.

There were a great number of Portuguese vessels lying at Rio de Janeiro at this time. No accounts had been received from Lisbon for six months, and it was believed the French had taken Portugal. I counted every day we remained as so much of my time lost, and wearied very much. At length a ship arrived from Lisbon and all the Portuguese prepared to sail. The governor's linguist came on board the *Amelia* and requested, as a personal favour, that Captain Shiels would allow four of his men to go on board the Commodore to assist in the voyage home, as it would be a winter's passage.

I immediately volunteered. I hoped by this means to reach England sooner and obtain more money for Sarah, as I would receive a full share of the *Amelia* in England the same as if I had continued in her. Had I know the delays, the fatigue and vexations I was to endure from these execrable superstitious Portuguese sailors, I never would have left the *Amelia* for any reward the Commodore could have given me—and he was very kind to us. He knew our value, and his whole reliance was upon us. We were to work the ship, and

fight the ship should an enemy lay us alongside. He
had been forty years trading between Lisbon and Rio
de Janeiro, and in all that time never had made a winter's voyage.

The Portuguese are the worst sailors in the world
in rough or cold weather, and we had plenty of both,
but worse than all we had a black fellow of a priest
on board to whom the crew paid more attention than
the captain. He was for ever ringing his bell for mass
and sprinkling holy water upon the men. Whenever
it blew harder than ordinary they were sure to run to
the quarterdeck to the black priest. We were almost
foundered at one time by this unseamanlike conduct.
The whole crew ran to the quarterdeck, kneeling
down, resigned to their fate, the priest sprinkling holy
water most profusely upon them, while we four Englishmen were left to steer the vessel and hand the sails.
It required two of the four to steer, so that there were
only two to hand the sails. The consequence was she
broached to. William Mercer and I ran and cut the
foregeers, and allowed the yard to swing. At the same
time, the captain, mate and boatswain hauled in the
forebrace and she righted in a moment. Had her
commons not been very high, she must have filled
while she lay upon her beam ends. The sea was all
over her deck round the hatch, but so soon as she
righted and we were going to make sail the Portuguese left their priest and lent us a hand.

We were wrought almost to death and never could
have made out the voyage had we not been well fed

and the captain given us plenty of liquor. The black priest rung his bell at his stated time whatever we were doing, and the Portuguese would run to their berths for their crosses. Often the main tack was left half hauled aboard at the sound of his bell, and the vessel left to drift leeward until prayers were over. As two men could do nothing to the sail when the wind was fresh, after prayers they would return and begin bawling and hauling, calling upon their saints as if they would come to assist.

We were thus almost driven to distraction by them and could scarce keep off our hands from boxing their ears. Many a hearty curse they and their saints got. Then they would run to the captain or priest and make complaint that the Englishmen had cursed Saint Antonio or some other of the saints. I often wondered the captain did not confine the priest to his cabin in foul weather, as he was sure to be busiest then. When they complained, the captain took our part and over-awed the Portuguese, or I really believe they would have thrown us overboard. They often looked at us as if they could have eat us without salt, and told us to our face we were 'star pork', that is, all the same as swine—that we knew nothing of God or the saints.

I showed them my Bible and the names of the saints. They were quite surprised. Had I made another voyage I would have made converts of many of them. I was bald headed and they called me an English padre. Often the bell rang while we were at dinner. They inquired why I would not go to mass. 'I mess

with the Coussinero,' I replied.* They began to think
I had the best religion. They seemed to think the foul
weather was all upon our account, and the virgin and
saints sent it because they employed heretics on board.

We had a supercargo on board as passenger, who
had made his fortune in the slave trade and was
returning home to Portugal. He took unwell and died.
At his funeral there were the following manoeuvres
gone through. Everyone had a candle in his hand, and
all stood in a double line upon the deck. There were
even lanthorns hung over the ship's side to light him
to the bottom. The body was carried along the double
line, the priest chanting, and every one touched him
before he was thrown overboard. The captain
requested us to do as the others did. Says Will
Mercer, 'Captain, I will throw him overboard for you,
if you please.'

At length, after a tedious voyage of three months,
I got out of this vile crew. When we reached the
Tagus the Portuguese began to quarrel and knock us
about.** We stood our ground the best way we could
until the captain got five of them sent on shore under
a guard of soldiers. We remained at the captain's
house until we got our wages. The owners gave us a
doubloon a piece over and above our agreement for
saving the ship, as the captain did us every justice to
the owners at the time, saying, 'If the English were as

* Coussinero: cook.
** The Tagus is the estuary Lisbon is situated on.

careful of their souls as they are of their bodies, they would be the best people in the world.'

I had many conversations with the captain concerning the ignorance of the Portuguese people in general, and asked why the priest did not inform them better. He said, 'Were we to inform them they would soon turn the priest about his business and rise against the government. They must only get knowledge little by little.'

We assisted at a religious ceremony before we came away, at the special request of our kind friend the captain. The foresail that was set when she broached to was given as an offering to the church, as the black priest told them it was through it they were saved. Although the worst sailor in the world knew it was the sail that would have sunk us, they dared not contradict the priest. The whole ship's crew carried it through the streets of Lisbon upon handkerchiefs to the church where it was placed upon the altar with much mummery. We came away and left them but the owners of the vessel bought back the sail again, after the priests had blessed it to their minds, as the church had more use for money than foresails.

William Mercer and I entered on board a brig bound for London, which was to sail in a few days, during which time we rambled about through the filthy streets of Lisbon. The higher orders of the Portuguese are very kind and civil. I was too late one evening to get on board the brig. A Portuguese merchant noticed my perplexity, for it is no pleasing thing to have a lodging to seek in Lisbon at a latish hour. Without my requesting him, he took me to his own house, gave me an excellent supper and bed. Had I been a gentleman of his acquaintance he could not have been kinder or paid me more attention. He ordered his servant to call me at any hour in the morning I chose.

As war was now looked for we were afraid for the press.* The Portuguese captain, at our request, got each of us a protection from the British consul at Lisbon. With a joyful heart I set sail for London to look out for an Indiaman that I might get to Bombay and inquire for Sarah, for she was still the idol of all my affections. At this time I was all anxiety to reach England. I often hoped she had reached her father's house and there was pining at my absence. I used for days to flatter myself with these dreams.

When we arrived at Gravesend a man-of-war's boat came on board to press any Englishmen there might be on board. William and I did not choose to trust to our protections now that we were in the river. So we stowed ourselves away among some bags of cotton where we were almost smothered but could hear every word that was said. The captain told the lieutenant he had no more hands than he saw, and they were all Portuguese. The lieutenant was not very particular, and left the brig without making much search.

* Britain had by now entered the French Revolutionary Wars.

When the boat left the vessel we crept from our hiding hole, and not long after a custom-house officer came on board. When we cast anchor, as I had a suit of long clothes in my chest that I had provided, should I have been so fortunate as have found Sarah at Port Jackson, to dash away with her a bit on shore, I put them on immediately and gave the custom-house officer half a guinea for the loan of his cocked hat and powdered wig. The long gilt-headed cane was included in the bargain.

I got a waterman to put me on shore. I am confident my own father, had he been alive, could not have known me with my cane in my hand, cocked hat and bushy wig. I inquired at the waterman the way to the inn where the coach set out from for London; I at the same time knew as well as him. I passed for a passenger. At the inn I called for a pint of wine, pens and ink, and was busy writing any nonsense that came in my head until the coach set off. All these precautions were necessary. Had the waterman suspected me to be a sailor he would have informed the press-gang in one minute. The waiters at the inn would have done the same.

By these precautions I arrived safe in London but did not go down to Wapping until next day, where I took up my old lodgings, still in my disguise. My landlord went on board and brought on shore my bedding and chest. I left them under his charge while I went to Lincoln to Sarah's parents where I made every inquiry—but they knew not so much of her as I did myself. The last information they had obtained was from the letter I had put in the post office for them before I sailed in the *Amelia*.

I immediately returned to London where, to my disappointment, I found there was not a berth to be got in any of the Indiamen who were for Bombay direct. They were all full. I then, as my next best, went to be engaged as cooper on board the *Nottingham* for China direct, depending on providence if we were ever to meet again. To find some way to effect my purpose, my landlord took me to be impressed. He got the six guineas allowed the bringer, which he returned to me. He was from Inverness, as honest a man as ever lived. I had always boarded in his house when in London.

A curious scene happened at my entry. There were a few more impressed on the same day, one an old tar. When asked by Captain Rogers, in his examination, how they hauled the main tack aboard, he replied, 'I can't tell, your honour, but I can show.' He clapped his foot into Captain Rogers' pocket, at the same instant leaped on his shoulders, tore his coat to the skirts, saying, 'Thus we haul it aboard.'

Captain Barefoot of the *Nottingham* and the other captains laughed heartily, as well as Rogers, who said rather peevishly, 'You might have shown, without tearing my coat.'

'How could I, your honour?' was the reply.*

* Perhaps this was the only means the old tar had of showing his displeasure at being pressed.

12

Arrival at the Cape of Good Hope—
Singular Incident—Java—
Wampoa—Chinese Artificers—
Music—Returns to England, and is
Impressed—Leith Roads—Mutiny—
Storm at Sea.

I THUS AGAIN set off as cooper of the *Nottingham* in 1793. Nothing worthy of notice happened. As I have gone over the same voyage before I will not detain the reader, but one circumstance that I witnessed off the Cape of Good Hope I cannot avoid mentioning as a dreadful example of what man will dare, and the perils he will encounter, to free himself from a situation he dislikes.

A man-of-war had been washing her gratings when the India fleet hove in sight. (They are washed by being lowered overboard and allowed to float astern.) Four or five men had slipped down upon them, cut them adrift and were thus voluntarily committed to the vast Atlantic without a bit of biscuit or a drop of water or any means of guiding the gratings they were floating upon in the hope of being picked up by some vessel. They held out their arms to us and supplicated in the wildest manner to be taken on board.

The captain would not. The *Nottingham* was a fast sailing ship and the first in the fleet. He said, 'I will not. Some of the stern ships will pick them up.' While he spoke these unfortunate and desponding fellow creatures lessened to our view, while their cries rung in our ears. I hope some of the stern ships picked them up. Few things I have seen are more strongly impressed upon my memory than the despairing looks and frantic gestures of these victims in quest of liberty. Next morning the frigate they had left came alongside of us and inquired if we had seen them. The captain gave an indirect answer to their inquiries, as well he might.

When we arrived at Java and anchored at Batavia I made every inquiry for a country ship, and would have left the *Nottingham* in a moment had there been one.* All my money was concealed upon my person for a start. I thought of falling sick and remaining until a country ship came, but I might really have become what I feigned in this European's grave, as I must have remained in the hospital. Had I walked about the city in health, the Dutch would soon have kidnapped me. I was thus once more baffled.

Indeed, I must confess, I did not feel the same anguish now I had endured before. It was now four years since I had left her in the colony, and her leaving it so soon, without waiting for me, showed she cared less about me than I cared for her. Not to write to her parents I had often thought very neglectful of her. I made up my mind not to leave the *Nottingham* at such risks, but to return in her to England and settle, as I had now some cash and had seen all I could see, and just make one more call at her friends in Lincoln, in my way to Scotland, and be ruled by the information I there obtained.

We sailed for Wampoa, where I was kindly received by my Chinese friends. I now paid more attention and saw things without the glare of novelty and have no cause to alter anything I said before. I had always, while at home, thought them the best tradesmen and most ingenious of people. I am

* Batavia: Jakarta.

inclined to think they have been overrated in regard to their abilities. Some things they do very neat, but considering the things they have to do them with it is no wonder. I mean their varnishes and colours, native productions.

Let the following facts that I can vouch for speak for themselves. In my own line they are unable to make any article with two ends, such as barrels. They have only reached the length of a tub. These they dool, that is pin with bamboos, the joints of the staves as well as the bottom. When a cask that comes from Europe is to be broached they cannot even bore and place the crane on it. A foreign cooper must go on shore and do it. Many a half dollar I have got for this service myself from the Chinese merchants.

I do not believe they can make a nail with a head. Many thousand of their nails I have had through my hands, and never saw one with a head upon it such as we have in England. Their nails are either sprigs or simply bent like a crow's toe. They are the worst smiths of any people, and can do nothing with a bar of iron if thick. I and the other coopers always kept the cuttings of our hoops which they bought with avidity—but larger pieces they would scarce take from us.

A vessel, the *Argyll*, while we were there in the *King George*, had lost her rudder in the voyage out and could not sail without a new one. There was not a smith in Canton who could forge the ironwork. The captain of the ship applied to the armourer of the *King*

George who took it in hand and in three weeks gained one hundred dollars by the job.

They appear to me to be excellent copiers, but not inventors. One of our officers sat for a painter to draw his picture and told the Chinese not to make him ugly. 'How can make other than is?' was the reply. He had no idea of altering a single feature to add to the looks of the object he was painting. All was a slavish copy of what was before his eyes. If you want anything made out of the common they must have one of the same as a pattern or they will not take it in hand. And what is further proof of their want of invention is, when you see one house you have seen every house of the same rank, or any other articles of their manufacture you have seen all. There is scarcely any variety and you need give yourself no trouble looking for others if the price pleases.

There is no change of fashion: the oldest articles you can fall in with are the same make and fashion as the newest, and a traveller who visited the country two hundred years ago could know no difference but in the men. They would be new, the old having died; the present race, I may say, wearing their dress and inhabiting their houses without the least change in the general appearance.

The only instrument of music I saw was a bagpipe, like the small Lowland pipe, on which they play well. Their gongs cannot be called a musical instrument. When John Tuck, the deputy emperor, appears (he is called so by the seamen on account of his having a gallows on board the grand boat which is as large as a seventy-four-gun ship and crowded with attendants), his band consists only of bagpipes. Their gongs are only used that I heard to make *tchin*, *tchin* to Joss in bad weather and at their paper sacrifices; and every vessel, down to the smallest sampan, has a Joss on board.

The deputy emperor comes once every year to view the fleet and pay his respects to the commodore. It is the grandest sight upon the river. Not so much as a sampan is allowed to move. He makes a present to every ship in the fleet of bullocks, wine, schamsee and flour. The officers start the schamsee overboard—it is a pernicious liquor distilled from rice. The flour is so coarse it is given to the hogs.

They measure every ship and can tell to a quarter chest how much she will hold. The first American sloop that came, she having only one mast, the Chinamen said, 'Hey, yaw, what fashion? How can measure ship with one mast?'—they having been accustomed to measure ships with more masts than one. They measure between the masts the breadth and depth of the ship.

I went up the river to the Dutch Folly, a fort lying waste opposite Canton in the middle of the river. The Dutch pretended they wished to build an hospital for their sick and got leave to do so, but their design was discovered by the bursting of a large barrel full of shot, and the Chinese put a stop to their undertaking, which now lies waste.

The Chinese sell all their fish, frogs, rats and hogs alive, and all by weight. Their frogs are bred and fed by them and are the largest I ever saw. When we bought our sea stock the hogs came on board in the baskets in which they were weighed.

The Chinese women are seldom seen in the streets. They walk very ill, and their gowns sweep the ground. Their hair is very prettily done up in the form of a crown on the top of their heads and fastened with a large gold or silver pin. The Tartar women are to be met at every step.

The cargo being complete, we fell down the river using our old precaution to keep off the Chinese chop-officers, and they retired with the same exclamation, 'Hey, yaw, what fashion? Too much baubry. Too much baubry.'

Nothing uncommon happened until we reached the Downs. I had allowed my beard to grow long and myself to be very dirty to be as unlikely as possible when the man-of-war boats came on board to press the crew. As we expected, they came. I was in the hold, sorting among the water casks, and escaped. They took every hand that would answer. I rejoiced in my escape but my joy was of short duration. One of the men they had taken had a sore leg. The boat brought him back—and I had the bad luck to be taken and he was left. Thus were all my schemes blown into the air.

I found myself in a situation I could not leave, a bondage that had been imposed upon me against my

will, and no hopes of relief until the end of the war—
not that I disliked it, but I had now become weary of
wandering for a time and longed to see Scotland
again. My heart always pointed to my native land.
Remonstrance and complaint were equally vain.

I therefore made up my mind to it, and was as
happy as a man in blasted prospects can be. I was
taken on board the *Venerable*, Admiral Duncan. She
was the flagship and commanded by Captain Hope,
now Admiral Hope. The *Venerable's* boats had made
a clean ship of the *Nottingham*. She was forced to be
brought up the river by ticket-porters and old Greenwich men. Next morning sixty of us who had
belonged to the *Nottingham* were turned over to the
Edgar, seventy-four, Captain Sir Charles Henry
Knowles. This was on the 11th June 1794. I was
stationed in the gunner's crew.

We went upon a cruise to the coast of Norway,
then touched at Shetland for fresh provisions. Afterwards we sailed for Leith Roads. I now felt all the
inconveniencies of my confinement. I was at home in
sight of the place where I wished all my wanderings
to cease. Captain Barefoot of the *Nottingham* had
wrote to Sir C. H. Knowles in my behalf, and he was
very kind to me. I asked leave to go on shore to see
my friends which he consented to, but Lieutenant
Collis would not allow me, saying 'it was not safe to
allow a pressed man to go on shore at his native place'.

Had I been allowed, I did not intend to leave the
Edgar. I would not have run away for any money,

upon my kind captain's account. My uncle came on board and saw me before we sailed, and I was visited by my other friends, which made me quite happy.

While we lay in Leith Roads, a mutiny broke out in the *Defiance*, seventy-four. The cause was, their captain gave them five-water grog; now the common thing is three-waters. The weather was cold. The spirit thus reduced was, as the mutineers called it, as thin as muslin and quite unfit to keep out the cold. No seaman could endure this in cold climates. Had they been in hot latitudes they would have been happy to get it thus for the sake of the water, but then they would not have got it.

The *Edgar* was ordered alongside the *Defiance* to engage her, if necessary, to bring her to order. We were saved this dreadful alternative by their returning to duty. She was manned principally by fishermen, stout resolute dogs. When bearing down upon her my heart felt so sad and heavy, not that I feared death or wounds, but to fight my brother, as it were. I do not believe the *Edgar's* crew would have manned the guns. They thought the *Defiance* men were in the right, and had they engaged us heartily as we would have done a French seventy-four, we could have done no good, only blown each other out of the water, for the ships were of equal force; and if there were any odds the *Defiance* had it in point of crew. Had I received my discharge and one hundred guineas I could not have felt my heart lighter than I did when we returned to our anchorage. And the gloom immediately vanished from every face in the ship.

We shortly after sailed on a cruise in the north seas and encountered a dreadful gale on the 17th October. I never was in such danger in all my life. The *Edgar* was only newly put in commission, and her rigging was new and not properly seasoned. We in a few hours carried away our bowsprit and foremast in this dreadful night, then our mizen and main topmast. With great difficulty we cut them clear. Soon after our mainmast loosened in the step, and we every moment expected it to go through her bottom. Then no exertion could have saved us from destruction. The carpenter, by good fortune, got it secured.

We lost all our anchors and cables in our attempts to bring her to, save one. At length it moderated a little, when we rigged jury masts and made for the Humber where we brought to with our only remaining anchor—when the *Inflexible*, Captain Savage, hove in sight and took us in tow. When in this situation the coasters, as they passed, called to the *Inflexible*, 'What prize have you got in tow?' A fresh gale sprung up and the *Inflexible* was forced to cast us off.

The weather moderated again and we proceeded up the Swain the best way we could into Blackstakes, Chatham. My berth during the storm, as one of the gunner's crew, was in charge of the powder on deck we used in firing our guns of distress. The ship rolled so much we were often upon our beam ends, and rolled a number of our guns overboard. We were forced to start all our beer and water to lighten the ship, but we rode it out, contrary to our expectation, and were shortly after turned over, captain and all, to the *Goliah*, seventy-four guns, and sailed to join Sir John Jervis in the blockade of Toulon. We boarded a Spanish ship and found on board thirty Austrian prisoners. They every man entered with us as marines.

13

Action off Cape St Vincent—
Blockade of Cadiz—Action at
Aboukir Bay—Anecdotes of the
Battle—Subsequent Occurrences—
Landing of the British Army in
Egypt—Ophthalmia—Return to
England.

WE NEXT SAILED for St Forensa Bay in the island of Corsica to water, but found the French in possession of the watering-place, and could get none. I belonged to the launch and had charge of the powder and match. I was constantly on shore when any service was to be done in destroying stores, spiking guns, blowing up batteries, and enjoyed it much. We carried off all the brass guns, and those metal ones that were near the edge of the rocks we threw into the sea. This was excellent sport to us but we were forced to leave it and sail to Gibraltar for water and provisions; but could obtain no supplies and sailed for Lisbon where we got plenty, having been on short allowance for some time before.

While we lay at Lisbon we got private intelligence overland that the Spanish fleet was at sea. We with all dispatch set sail in pursuit of them. We were so fortunate as come in sight of them by break of day, on the 14th of February, off Cape St Vincent. They consisted of twenty-five sail, mostly three-deckers. We were only eighteen but we were English, and we gave them their valentines in style.

Soon as we came in sight, a bustle commenced not to be conceived or described. To do it justice, while every man was as busy as he could be the greater order prevailed. A serious cast was to be perceived on every face but not a shade of doubt or fear. We rejoiced in a general action; not that we loved fighting, but we all wished to be free to return to our homes and follow our own pursuits. We knew there was no other way

of obtaining this than by defeating the enemy. 'The
hotter war the sooner peace,' was a saying with us.
When everything was cleared, the ports open, the
matches lighted and guns run out, then we gave them
three such cheers as are only to be heard in a British
man-of-war. This intimidates the enemy more than a
broadside, as they have often declared to me. It shows
them all is right, and the men in the true spirit baying
to be at them.

During the action, my situation was not one of
danger but most wounding to my feelings and trying
to my patience. I was stationed in the after-magazine,
serving powder from the screen, and could see
nothing—but I could feel every shot that struck the
Goliah, and the cries and groans of the wounded were
most distressing as there was only the thickness of the
blankets of the screen between me and them. Busy as
I was, the time hung upon me with a dreary weight.
Not a soul spoke to me but the master-at-arms as he
went his rounds to inquire if all was safe. No sick
person ever longed more for his physician than I for
the voice of the master-at-arms. The surgeon's-mate
at the commencement of the action spoke a little, but
his hands were soon too full of his own affairs.

Those who were carrying run like wild creatures
and scarce opened their lips. I would far rather have
been on the decks amid the bustle, for there the time
flew on eagle's wings. The *Goliah* was sore beset; for
some time she had two three-deckers upon her. The
men stood to their guns as cool as if they had been

exercising. The admiral ordered the *Britannia* to our assistance. Iron-sides, with her forty-twos, soon made them sheer off.† Towards the close of the action the men were very weary. One lad put his head out of the porthole, saying, 'Damn them, are they not going to strike yet?' For us to strike was out of the question.

At length the roar of the guns ceased and I came on deck to see the effects of a great sea engagement—but such a scene of blood and desolation I want words to express. I had been in a great number of actions with single ships in the *Proteus* and *Surprise* during the seven years I was in them. This was my first action in a fleet and I had only a small share in it. We had destroyed a great number and secured four three-deckers. One they had the impiety to call the *Holy Ghost* we wished much to get, but they towed her off. The fleet was in such a shattered situation we lay twenty-four hours in sight of them, repairing our rigging.

It is after the action the disagreeable part commences. The crews are wrought to the utmost of their strength. For days they have no remission of their toil, repairing the rigging and other parts injured in the action. Their spirits are broke by fatigue. They have no leisure to talk of the battle and, when the usual

---

† The *Britannia* is a first-rate, carrying 110 guns. She was the only ship that carried forty-two-pounders on her lower deck, and thirty-two on her middle deck. She was the strongest built ship in the navy. The sailors upon this account called her 'Iron-Sides'.

round of duty returns, we do not choose to revert to a disagreeable subject. Who can speak of what he did where all did their utmost? One of my mess-mates had the heel of his shoe shot off. The skin was not broke yet his leg swelled and became black. He was lame for a long time.

On our return to Lisbon we lost one of the fleet, the *Bombay Castle*. She was stranded and completely lost. All her crew were saved. We were in great danger in the *Goliah*. Captain Sir C. H. Knowles was tried for not lending assistance, when he needed it himself. The court-martial honourably acquitted him. Collis, our first lieutenant, told us not to cheer when he came on board, but we loved our captain too well to be restrained. We had agreed upon a signal with the cox-swain, if he was, as he ought to be, honourably acquitted. The signal was given and in vain Collis forbade. We manned the yards and gave three hearty cheers. Not a man on board but would have bled for Sir C. H. Knowles. To our regret we lost him to our ship at this very time. He was as good a captain as I ever sailed with. He was made admiral, and went home in the *Britannia*.

Captain Foley took command of the *Goliah* and we joined the blockade of Cadiz where we remained, sending our boat to assist at the bombardments and covering them, until Admiral Nelson came out again and picked out thirteen seventy-fours from the fleet. The *Goliah* was one. She was the fastest sailing ship in the fleet. We did not stay to water but got a supply from the ships that were to remain, and away we set under a press of sail, not knowing where.

We came to an anchor in the Straits of Messina. There was an American man-of-war at anchor. Captain Foley ordered him to unmoor that the *Goliah* might get her station, as it was a good one near the shore, but Jonathan would not budge, but made answer, 'I will let you know I belong to the United States of America and I will not give way to any nation under the sun but in a good cause.'*

So we came to an anchor where we could. We remained here but a short time when we got intelligence that the French fleet were up the Straits. We then made sail for Egypt but missed them, and came back to Syracuse and watered in twenty-four hours. I was up all night filling water. The day after we left Syracuse we fell in with a French brig who had just left the fleet. Admiral Nelson took her in tow and she conducted us to where they lay at anchor in Aboukir Bay.**

We had our anchors out at our stern port with a spring upon them, and the cable carried along the ship's side, so that the anchors were at our bows, as if there was no change in the arrangement. This was to prevent the ships from swinging round, as every ship was to be brought to by her stern. We ran in between the French fleet and the shore to prevent any

---

* Jonathan: A generic name for an American.
** Aboukir Bay: near Alexandria in Egypt.

communication between the enemy and the shore. Soon as they were in sight a signal was made from the admiral's ship for every vessel as she came up to make the best of her way, firing upon the French ships as she passed, and 'every man to take his bird' as we joking called it.

The *Goliah* led the van. There was a French frigate right in our way. Captain Foley cried, 'Sink that brute, what does he there?' In a moment she went to the bottom and her crew were seen running into her rigging. The sun was just setting as we went into the bay, and a red and fiery sun it was. I would, if had I had my choice, been on the deck. There I would have seen what was passing and the time would not have hung so heavy, but every man does his duty with spirit, whether his station be in the slaughterhouse or the magazine.†

I saw as little of this action as I did of the one on the 14th February off Cape St Vincent. My station was in the powder magazine with the gunner. As we entered the bay we stripped to our trousers, opened our ports, cleared, and every ship we passed gave them a broadside and three cheers. Any information we got was from the boys and women who carried the powder. The women behaved as well as the men, and got a present for their bravery from the grand signior.

---

† The seamen call the lower deck near the mainmast the slaughterhouse, as it is amidships and the enemy aim their fire principally at the body of the ship.

When the French admiral's ship blew up, the
Goliah got such a shake we thought the after-part of
her had blown up until the boys told us what it was.
They brought us every now and then the cheering
news of another French ship having struck, and we
answered the cheers on deck with heartfelt joy. In the
heat of the action a shot came right into the magazine
but did no harm as the carpenters plugged it up and
stopped the water that was rushing in.

I was much indebted to the gunner's wife who gave
her husband and me a drink of wine every now and
then, which lessened our fatigue much. There were
some of the women wounded, and one woman
belonging to Leith died of her wounds and was buried
on a small island in the bay. One woman bore a son
in the heat of the action. She belonged to Edinburgh.

When we ceased firing I went on deck to view the
state of the fleets, and an awful sight it was. The whole
bay was covered with dead bodies, mangled, wounded
and scorched, not a bit of clothes on them except their
trousers. There were a number of French, belonging
to the French admiral's ship the *L'Orient*, who had
swam to the *Goliah* and were cowering under her fore-
castle. Poor fellows, they were brought on board and
Captain Foley ordered them down to the steward's
room to get provisions and clothing.

One thing I observed in these Frenchmen quite
different from anything I had ever before observed.
In the American war, when we took a French ship,
the *Duke de Chartres*, the prisoners were as merry as

if they had taken us, only saying, '*Fortune de guerre*'—
you take me today, I take you tomorrow. Those we
now had on board were thankful for our kindness but
were sullen and as downcast as if each had lost a ship
of his own.

The only incidents I heard of are two. One lad who
was stationed by a salt box on which he sat to give out
cartridges and keep the lid close—it is a trying
berth—when asked for a cartridge, he gave none, yet
he sat upright. His eyes were open. One of the men
gave him a push. He fell all his length on the deck.
There was not a blemish on his body yet he was quite
dead, and was thrown overboard. The other, a lad
who had the match in his hand to fire his gun. In the
act of applying it a shot took off his arm. It hung by
a small piece of skin. The match fell to the deck. He
looked to his arm and, seeing what had happened,
seized the match in his left hand and fired off the gun
before he went to the cockpit to have it dressed. They
were in our mess or I might never have heard of it.
Two of the mess were killed and I knew not of it until
the day after. Thus terminated the glorious first of
August, the busiest night in my life.

Soon after the action the whole fleet set sail with
the prizes, and left the *Goliah* as guard ship. We
remained here until we were relieved by the *Tigre*,
seventy-four, when we sailed for Naples to refit. After
refitting we sailed for Malta to join in the blockade,
where we remained eight months without any occurrence worthy of notice. At length the *Goliah* became

so leaky we were forced to leave our station and sail for Gibraltar where, after watering, we sailed for England.

We got some marines from the Rock to reinforce the *Goliah's* complement—one of them a tall stout Englishman who had been cock of the Rock.* He was very overbearing. There are often quarrels at the ship's fires when the men are boiling their kettles. We had a stout little fellow of an Irishman, who had been long in the *Goliah*. The marine pushed his kettle aside. Paddy demanded why he did so.

'Because I choose to do it.'

'I won't allow you while the life is in me,' was the reply.

'Do you wish to fight?' said the Englishman.

'Yes, and I do,' said Paddy. 'I will take the Gibraltar rust out of you or you shall beat the life out of my body before we are done.'

A fight was made up in a minute, and they went well forward on the deck to be out of sight of the officers. To it they went and fought it out, we forming a ring and screening them from observation. Paddy was as good as his word, for he took the rust off the marine so well he was forced to give in, and we were all happy to see the lobster-back's pride taken out of him.

On our arrival she was put out of commission, and the crew turned over to the *Royal William*, the guard

* The Rock: Gibraltar.

ship, and had two or three days' liberty on shore by the admiral's order.

I was next drafted on board the *Ramilies* and sailed for Belleisle, but remained only a short time in her when I was turned over to the *Ajax*, Captain Alexander F. Cochrane, upon preferment.* We sailed for Ferrol and attempted to cut out some vessels but did not succeed, then stood for Algiers to water, having a fleet of transports with troops on board under convoy. The troops were commanded by Sir Ralph Abercromby. Having watered, we sailed with the army to Mamarice Bay, and the troops were encamped upon a fine piece of ground, with a rivulet running through the centre. The French had just left the place, having first done all the mischief in their power.

While we lay here an engineer named William Balcarras went in a frigate to reconnoitre the French works. He landed and, having attained his object, was coming off in his boat when he was followed by another from the shore and shot dead before he reached the frigate.

We left Mamarice Bay and sailed to Rhodes, where we took in forage for the cavalry. We then sailed for Alexandria and landed the troops.

I belonged to one of the boats. Captain A. F. Cochrane was beach-master, and had the ordering of the troops in the landing. We began to leave the ships about twelve o'clock and reached the shore about

* Belleisle is in the Bay of Biscay.

sunrise in the morning. We rowed very slow with our oars muffled. It was a pleasant night. The water was very still and all was as silent as death. No one spoke but each cast an anxious look to the shore, then at each other, impatient to land. Each boat carried about one hundred men and did not draw nine inches of water.

The French cavalry were ready to receive us, but we soon forced them back and landed eight thousand men the first morning. We had good sport at landing the troops as the Frenchmen made a stout resistance. We brought back the wounded men to the ships.

For some time we supplied the troops on shore with provisions and water. After the advance of the troops into the country I was with the seamen on shore, assisting at the siege of Alexandria and working like a labourer in cutting off the branch of the Nile that supplied the city with water. One of the *Ajax's* boats, at Sir Ralph Abercromby's request, carried him after receiving his wound, on board the hospital ship.

Of all the countries I was ever in, in all my wanderings, I could not remain in Egypt. The air is so dry and I felt so disagreeable. It is, on the whole, sandy and barren, yet what I saw of it that was cultivated is very agreeable. For some days before the town surrendered I had been so bad with the flux I was forced to go on board. After the town surrendered and the operations of the army ceased we sailed for Malta. At this time I was blind with the ophthalmia and continued thus for six weeks.

My sufferings were most acute. I could not lie down for a moment, for the scalding water that continually flowed from my eyes filled them and put me to exquisite torture. I sat constantly on my chest with a vessel of cold water bathing them. If I slept I awoke in an agony of pain. All the time the flux was most severe upon me and the surgeon would not dry it up, as it, he said, relieved my eyes. When we came to Malta a French surgeon cured me by touching the balls of my eyes with tincture of opium, but the pain of the application was very severe. Thank God, however, I soon after recovered my health and spirits.

From Malta we sailed to Gibraltar where we watered, then sailed for England where, to my joy, I found that peace was concluded. We were all paid off shortly after our arrival. I was ship's corporal when I was discharged.

14

*Author Arrives in Edinburgh—
Marries and Settles as a Cooper—
Forced to Leave his Business from
Danger of Impressment—Retires to
Cousland—Subsequent
Occurrences—Returns to Edinburgh
from Inability to Work at
Cousland—Failure of Prospects—
Present Situation.*

I WAS ONCE more my own master, and felt so happy I was like one bewildered. Did those on shore only experience half the sensations of a sailor at perfect liberty after being seven years on board ship without a will of his own, they would not blame his eccentricities but wonder he was not more foolish.

After a few days my cooler reason began to resume its power and I began to think what should be my after pursuits. It was now seven years since I had been pressed from the *Nottingham*. In that time the thoughts of Sarah had faded into a distant pleasing dream. The violent desire I at one time felt to repossess her was now softened into a curiosity to know what had become of her.

As I was now possessed of a good deal of pay and prize-money due, when I received it I went down by Lincoln to make inquiry, but no one had heard of her since I was there myself, nine years before. So all my inquiries after her terminated and I proceeded to Scotland, determined to settle, as I was now too old to undertake any more love pilgrimages after an individual, as I knew not in what quarter of the globe she was or whether she was dead or alive.

I arrived in Edinburgh just twenty-five years after I had left it to wander over the globe. I had been only twice there, once at the end of the American war when I found my father dead and my brothers wanderers. After my return from the voyage with Captain Portlock I remained only a few days and just passed through the city. When in the *Edgar*, I never had been on shore.

I scarce knew a face in Edinburgh. It had doubled itself in my absence. I now wandered in elegant streets where I had left corn growing. Everything was new to me. I confess I felt more sincere pleasure and enjoyment in beholding the beauties of Edinburgh than ever I felt in any foreign clime, for I now could identify myself with them. I was a Scotchman and I felt as if they were my own property. In China, in Naples, in Rio de Janeiro or even in London I felt as a stranger, and I beheld with only the eye of curiosity.

Here I now looked on with the eye of a son who is witnessing the improvements of his father's house. Little did I at this time think I should wander in these very streets to pick up a few coals to warm my aged limbs! But everything is wisely ordered by that Power who has protected me in dangers when I thought not of Him.

I felt myself, for a few weeks after my arrival, not so very happy. As I had anticipated, there was scarcely a friend I had left that I knew again. The old were dead, the young had grown up to manhood and many were in foreign climes. The Firth of Forth which in my youth appeared a sea to my inexperienced mind, Arthur Seat and the neighbouring hills, now seemed dwindled to insignificance in comparison to what I had witnessed in foreign parts. Because they were my native scenery I felt hurt that any other country should possess more imposing objects of their kind. But they were Scotch and I loved them still.

I could not settle to work but wandered up and

down. At length I fell in with a cousin of my own. We had been playfellows and a friendly intimacy had continued until I went to sea. I fixed my affections on her and we were married. I gave her my solemn promise never again to go to sea during her life. I then thought sincerely of settling and following my trade. I bought a house in the Castle Hill and furnished it well, then laid in a stock of wood and tools. I had as much work as I could do for a soap work at the Queensferry. For one year my prospects were as good as I could have wished, and I was as happy as ever I had been in my life.

But in a few months after the war broke out again and the press-gang came in quest of me.* I could no longer remain in Edinburgh and avoid them. My wife was like a distracted woman and gave me no rest until I sold off my stock in trade and the greater part of my furniture and retired to the country. Even until I got this accomplished I dared not to sleep in my own house, as I had more than one call from the gang.

I went to Cousland, nine miles from Edinburgh in the parish of Cranstoun, and put up at one Robert Moodie's, a small public house, not knowing what was to be my next pursuit. I could obtain no employment as a cooper unless I lived in a large or seaport town, and there I could not remain. I at length applied to Mr Dickson and got work from him at the lime quarries. My berth was to bore and charge the stones with

* Britain had entered the Napoleonic Wars.

gunpowder to facilitate the work. I continued to live at Robert Moodie's, my wife Margaret paying me an occasional visit, until I got a house of my own from Mr Dickson, when she came out to reside constantly with me.

I hoped that every month would put a period to the war and I would be allowed to return to Edinburgh. But peace still seemed to recede from Britain. Year after year I looked for it in vain. When the weather was good, night after night have I sat after my day's labour by the old windmill in Bartholomew's field, first gazing upon Edinburgh that I dared not reside in, then upon the vessels that glided along the Forth. A sigh would escape me at my present lot. My promise to Margaret kept me from them (my word has ever been my bond) or I should assuredly have gone to sea again. I was like a bird in a cage, with objects that I desired on every side but could not obtain.

The cultivation of the small garden attached to my cottage occupied my mind for some time. I was becoming a little more reconciled to my lot when the press-gang came out even to Cousland and took away a neighbour of the name of Murray. He had a large family and, through the interest of the minister and neighbouring gentlemen, he got off. His impressment was a great blow to my tranquillity for many months. For a long time I slept every night either in Dalkeith or Musselburgh, and during the day a stranger could not appear near the quarry without causing the most disagreeable sensations to me. At length this cause of uneasiness wore off likewise, and I settled down to my usual calm expectations of peace—but year followed year and my prospects were unaltered.

I now began to see the great alterations that had taken place in the country from the time I had been in it, when a boy, about the year 1766. At that time I had resided for some time with my uncle at Edmonstone. The country was very little inclosed. The farmers lived with their servants. Now the country was inclosed and the farmers were gentlemen.*

At Dalkeith fair, when the crops were off the ground, it was called 'long halter time'. The cattle during the fair got leave to stray at large while the farmers, their wives, daughters and servants were all at the fair, only one woman being left at home. Now the farmers, if they went to the fair, it was to sell or buy, not to make merry. Their wives and daughters would have thought themselves disgraced if they were seen at the fair. They no longer messed with their servants but lived like noblemen by themselves. If a servant had occasion to speak to his master, he must address him as if he had been an admiral—this to me appeared strange at first.

As Mr Dickson knew I was anxious for the news, he was so kind as give me a reading of the newspapers when he was done. The other workmen assembled in

---

* Inclosing was the annexing of common fields, meadows and pastures into consolidated farms.

my cottage on the evenings I got them and I read aloud. Then we would discuss the important parts together. The others were not friendly to the government, save one, an old soldier who had been in the East Indies. He and I always sided together. I had broke His Majesty's bread for fourteen years and would not, upon that account, hear his government spoken against.

I had but poor help from the old soldier and I had them all to contend with, but when I was like to be run down I bothered them with latitudes and longitudes and the old soldier swore to all I said and we contrived to keep our ground, for we had both been great travellers. When they spoke of heavy taxes I talked of China. When they complained of hard times I told them of West Indian slaves—but neither could make any impression on the other.

When Murray was pressed and I was forced to skulk like a thief, they thought they had a great triumph over me and did not spare their taunts. One would ask what I thought of British freedom; another if I could defend a government which did such things?

I was at no loss for my answer. I told them, 'Necessity had no law.' Could the government make perfect seamen as easily as they could soldiers there would be no such thing as pressing of seamen, and that I was happy to be of more value than them all put together, for they would not impress any of them, they were of so little value compared with me.

When the news of the victory of Trafalgar arrived

I had my triumph over them in return. None but an old tar can feel the joy I felt. I wrought none the next day but walked about enjoying the feeling of triumph. Every now and then I felt the greatest desire to hurra aloud, and many an hurra my heart gave that my mouth uttered not.

For eleven years I lived at Cousland. Year followed year, but still no views of peace. I grew old apace and the work became too heavy for me. I was now fifty-eight years of age, and they would not have taken me had I wished to enter the service. I therefore removed to Edinburgh, and again began to work for myself. My first employers had failed in business long before. The times were completely changed. I could not get constant employment for myself. I therefore wrought for any of the other masters who were throng, but the cooper business is so very poor I have been oftener out of employment than at work. Few of them keep journeymen. They, like myself, do all their work with their own hands.

I never had any children by my cousin during the seventeen years we lived together. Margaret during all that time never gave me a bad word or made any strife by her temper—but all have their faults. I will not complain, but more money going out than I by my industry could bring in has now reduced me to want in my old age.

At her death, which happened four years ago, I was forced to sell all my property except a small room in which I live, and a cellar where I do any little work I am so fortunate as obtain. This I did to pay the expenses of her funeral and a number of debts that had been contracted unknown to me. As my poverty will not allow me to pay for a seat in a church, I go in the evenings to the Little Church, but my house is in the Tolbooth parish.

Doctor Davidson visits me in his ministerial capacity. These, I may say, are the only glimpses of sunshine that ever visit my humble dwelling. Mr Mackenzie, my elder, is very attentive in giving me tickets of admission to the sermons that are preached in the school house in the Castle Hill. In one of Doctor Davidson's visits, he made me a present of a few shillings. It was a great gift from God. I had not one penny at the time in the house.

In the month of August, last year, a cousin of my own made me a present of as much money as carried me to London. I sailed in the *Hawk*, London smack. I was only a steerage passenger but fared as well as the cabin passengers. I was held constantly in tow by the passengers. My spirits were up. I was at sea again. I had not trode a deck for twenty years before. I had always a crowd round me listening to my accounts of the former voyages that I had made. Everyone was more kind to me than another. I was very happy.

Upon my arrival in London I waited upon my old captain, Portlock, but fortune was now completely against me. He had been dead six weeks before my arrival. I left the house, my spirits sunk with grief for his death and my own disappointment, as my chief dependence was upon his aid. I then went to Somerset House for the certificate of my service: seven years in the *Proteus* and *Surprise* in the American War, and seven in the *Edgar*, *Goliah*, *Ramilies* and *Ajax* in the French War.

I was ordered to go to the Admiralty Office first and then come back to Somerset House. When I applied at the Admiralty Office a clerk told me I had been too long of applying. I then went down to the Governor of Greenwich Hospital. I was not acquainted with him, but I knew the Governor of Greenwich would be a distressed seaman's friend. His servant told me he was in Scotland. I then waited upon Captain Gore whose son's life I had saved, but he was not at home. It was of no use to remain in London as my money wore down apace. I took my passage back to Edinburgh in the *Favourite*, London smack, and arrived just four weeks from my first setting out on this voyage of disappointment. What can I do? I must just take what fortune has still in store for me.

At one time, after I came home, I little thought I should ever require to apply for a pension, and therefore made no application until I really stood in need of it.

I eke out my subsistence in the best manner I can. Coffee made from the raspings of bread (which I obtain from the bakers) twice a day is my chief diet. A few potatoes or anything I can obtain with a few pence constitute my dinner. My only luxury is tobacco which I have used these forty-five years. To beg I never will submit. Could I have obtained a small pension for my past services, I should then have reached my utmost earthly wish and the approach of utter helplessness would not haunt me as it at present does in my solitary home. Should I be forced to sell it, all I would obtain could not keep me and pay for lodgings for one year. Then I must go to the poor's house, which God in his mercy forbid. I can look to my death bed with resignation but to the poor's house I cannot look with composure.

I have been a wanderer and the child of chance all my days, and now only look for the time when I shall enter my last ship, and be anchored with a green turf upon my breast, and I care not how soon the command is given.

SERVICE OF JOHN NICOL

SHIPS' NAMES.	WHERE.	PERIOD.
Proteus and *Surprise*	American War, West Indies	1776–83
Leviathan	Greenland	1784
Cotton Planter	West Indies	1784–85
King George	South Seas and China	1785–88
Lady Juliana	New South Wales and China	1789–91
Amelia	South Sea	1791–92
Nottingham	China	1793–94
Edgar, Goliah, Ramilies and *Ajax*	French War, Egypt, Mediterranean	1794–1801

Index

197